SOCCER DREAMS

.a

USA
1999 FIFA
WOMEN'S
WORLD CUP
CHAMPIONS

WORLD CUP

FIFA
For the Good of the Game

Leah Lauber

HEWLETT
PACKARD

Manufactured in the United States of America by Extra! Extra! Graphics, Inc., St. Petersburg, Florida

Library of Congress Catalog Card Number 2003112055

ISBN: 0-9745480-0-6
Editor/Photographer: Chris Lauber
Design Consultant: Rya Lauber
Interview Transcription: Nicole Lauber
Editorial Consultant: Patricia Lauber

Library of Congress Cataloging-in-Publication Data

Lauber, Leah F.
      Soccer Dreams: My true adventure following the U.S. Women's National Soccer Team, as a a fan and 12-year old Junior Reporter for the *St. Petersburg Times,* during the history-making 1999 FIFA Women's World Cup. -- First Edition

      ISBN 0-9745480-0-6 (paperback)
      1. Sports -- Women's Soccer 2. Journalism -- Sports I. Lauber, Leah, 1986 - II. Title.

      2003112055
      PCN

ATTENTION SOCCER ASSOCIATIONS AND EDUCATIONAL ORGANIZATIONS:
Quantity discounts are available on bulk purchases of this book for fund raising or educational purposes. Special editions can be created to fit specific needs.

For additional information, please contact:
WCI Press, Inc.
6967 Sunset Drive South
South Pasadena, Florida 33707
(727) 347-4440
fax: (727) 343-4804

Send Leah e-mail: WWCSoccerDreams@aol.com
Website: http://www.SoccerDreamsBook.com

Contents

Dedicated to

The past, present and future members of the U.S. Women's National Team. The past members created the foundation, the current members provide the inspiration, and the future members are on the fields across the United States, each with their own soccer dream.

Photography

How's this for a family project? I shot all the photos in Chapter 9 during a training session near Orlando, and a friendly game against Brazil the next day. I used my dad's equipment and he adjusted all the settings, but it was up to me to try to capture the action.

My dad, Chris Lauber, shot the vast majority of the photography in Soccer Dreams for our family photo albums. At the time, of course, he didn't know I would be writing this book. Though he has shot sports photography professionally for twenty years, most of the game action photos were taken from our seats in the stands. These show how I saw the games, as my dad was right next to me for each one.

And my grandfather, Papa Big Ed Lauber, took us to a game in Tampa against Finland and shot the photos of my sister, Nicole, and me with the members of the team in Chapter 3.

Only four photos in Soccer Dreams were shot by non-family members: Vernon Photography of Largo, FL provided the three portrait/team photos in Chapter 1. An unknown parent of one of my teammates gave us the photo of Michelle Demko, my dad and me in Chapter 1.

Thank You!

Gretchen Letterman, *St. Petersburg Times*, for all your support and guidance while I was a member of the X-Press Team; **Bryan Chenault,** U.S. Soccer, for your help in providing media credentials in Tampa and Orlando; **Aaron Heifetz,** 1999 FIFA Women's World Cup Organizing Committee for your help in providing media credentials during the tournament; **Jere Longman,** *New York Times*, for including me in your book, *The Girls of Summer.*

To all the **coaches and volunteers** who provide the opportunity for us kids to enjoy the sport of soccer, especially those at my club, Azalea Youth Soccer Association in St. Petersburg, Florida.

An extra special thank you to the members and coaches of the **U.S. Women's National Team,** who were always generous with their time, patient with us fans, and taught me, through their actions, to DREAM BIG. You are an inspiration!!

Finally, a giant thank you to all the members of my family, who have done so much for me in providing a great childhood and incredible experiences. Thank you for believing in my soccer dreams and your help in making them come true!

Section 1

Kicking Off

-1-
Love of The Game

When I was seven years old and signed up to play soccer for the first time, I knew I would like playing this great sport. For years, my family had been playing with soccer balls at the beach, but I had no idea of the many wonderful experiences I would enjoy playing and watching soccer.

How could I possibly know I would end up on the field, in the locker room, and under the press tent, not as a player, but as a junior reporter for the *St. Petersburg Times*, during the 1999 Women's World Cup? Back then, I didn't even know there was a Women's World Cup or a United States Women's National Team.

At registration, we went from line to line, turning in all the paperwork and paying the fees. Finally, we arrived at the volunteer sign-up table. My dad, who played in high school and college, but had never coached before, offered to be the assistant coach for our team, but since there weren't enough head coaches, he agreed to become our head coach. He's coached my teams every year since.

We wanted to enjoy soccer as a family, so my five year-old sister, Nicole, and I were on the same team with my dad as the coach. Nicole was pretty big for her age, but she was the youngest player on our under-eight team. The three of us, plus my mom, would load up the car every Saturday morning and we'd be off to another soccer adventure.

Trust me, every game was an adventure. In rec (recreational) soccer, there aren't tryouts like there are for club (or select) teams. Each player is assigned to a team, so it was often the luck of the draw if you found yourself on a strong or a weak team.

Let me tell you about my first team. Let's just say we were really young and not very good. We lost ten games and won just one. Back then, it was just fun with everyone chasing the ball, not really playing positions, your basic kick-and-run bunchball.

One girl on our team cried nearly every game, not because she was a baby, but because she just wouldn't give up. Kristen played so hard, often with minor injuries and tears flowing, but would keep on playing her heart out, never quitting until the game was over.

My sister, Nicole, said she wanted to play goalie and later even developed a real good punt until she broke the glass window in her bedroom. Once, this big girl came rushing toward Nicole with the ball at her feet, shot this rocket (for an eight-year old), and scored a powerful goal past Nicole.

From Top: My sister Nicole and me on the beach as toddlers, and with our dad, taking a goal kick and fighting for the ball in my first year.

Left: I'm all smiles on Trophy Day with my good friend, Jenelle McKee.
Below: During summer soccer, scoring my first - ever goal!!

Nicole started crying, because she froze and didn't know what to do. She didn't want to play goalie anymore, so my dad took her out of the game. A few minutes later, she had her cleats, socks and shinguards off. That same game, two of our teammates were stung by bees. We were both weak and unlucky.

The next year, Nicole didn't want to play, but I did. My second team was the Soccer Maniacs and we were quite good. Our record was 12-3 which was nearly the total opposite of the year before. We entered a club tournament, and although we lost two of the games, we won one against a club team. We were lucky with the draw that year. I learned how much more fun it is to play on a winning team than to play on a losing one.

My third year, our rec team was the Blizzards and we were awful. We had discipline problems, stupid stuff like girls going home with gum in their hair after waiting on line during shooting drills. We won just four games, but came back in our league tournament, winning the first two and playing our final game of the season with a gold medal at stake. Man was I nervous! We lost that day, but it sure was fun, playing for something important like a gold medal!

Then, I played co-ed summer soccer between my third and fourth years. I was one of three girls on an Under-10 co-ed team. Usually, I played defense on all my dad's teams, but my summer coach put me in at midfield. Once, I trapped the ball, dribbled twice and with a defender closing in on me, and with my right foot, I shot against two boys and I scored my very first goal. My dad was on the sidelines with his camera, and he caught a photo of my goal-scoring shot. I wonder how many players are fortunate enough to have a photo of their first-ever goal?

Now, the fourth year just blew all the other years away. With the luck of the draw, everything clicked. We were a great team, the Azalea Under-12 Red Knights. Our final record was 14 wins, one loss, and one tie. We dominated, outscoring our competition 55-10, with ten defensive shutouts.

Unfortunately, our only loss was in our league quarterfinals, knocking us right out of our undefeated run at the championship. I'm not making excuses but it was a terrible night. We were scheduled to start at 8:00 p.m. on a Saturday night, but there were four overtime games in a row, with penalty kicks, on our scheduled field.

Our field wasn't cleared until 9:15 p.m. and by the time we were ready to start at 9:30 p.m., it was already past most of my teammates' normal bedtime. Remember, we were eleven and twelve year old girls. Of course, so were the players on the other team.

Pinellas Park kicked off and somehow within the first minute, the ball trickled towards the goal, when one of our defenders whiffed at the ball and our goalie misplayed it. We're already down 1-0. But we fought back and tied it up in the first half, only to have the goal called off because the ref said the goalie was pushed into the goal with the ball. There wasn't anybody near the goalie when she stumbled into the goal with the ball. We tied it up for the second time in the second half and the ref let it stand, 1-1.

They scored again in the second half after a miskicked goal kick landed at an opponent's feet and she drilled the ball at the opposite post. We charged back to tie it up again late in the game, but ran out of steam in the first overtime and they scored on us twice. Down 4-2 at the whistle to end the first overtime, the other team started celebrating, our team started crying and my dad was calling us over to the bench.

But the ref insisted there was no time to take a break between overtime periods and ordered us back onto the field. Imagine playing an Under-12 quarterfinal match at 11:00 p.m. on a Saturday night and the ref wouldn't allow the standard five minute break to get some water, rest and encouragement from our coaches.

The Under-12 Red Knights was easily my BEST team. Sitting (L-R): Lauren Vogel, Alia Tovey, Chea Hott. Kneeling: Brittny Jensen, Leah Lauber, Morgan Bell, Jaime Knapp, Gina Fote. Standing: Assistant Coach John Piotti, Bridget Hennessy, Jackie Gentzel, Nicole Hawk, Amanda Tallent, Kathryn Piotti, Coach Chris Lauber, Assistant Coach Jack Tovey. Missing: Rachel Pomeroy, Alexis Searfoss

I also played three years for my school team, the St. Jude's Hawks.

Above: My skills really improved as a club player for Azalea Youth Soccer League.
Below: My dad, our assistant coach Michelle Demko and I after our season-ending region tournament.

Our whole team left it on the field that night in one of the most tiring, disappointing nights of my young life. When the final whistle blew to end the match and our season, my whole team was crying, including some of our parents. Me? Yeah, I cried nearly all the way home and again the next night.

Our dreams of an undefeated, championship season were over. We had an incredible run, almost magical, only to finish with the most bitter of defeats. I learned to never take anything for granted, especially a championship. What we would have done for a re-match. . .

What set that year apart was the great team chemistry we had. It was so good that most of us decided to stay together and become a club team the following year. But every season, every team starts fresh and some new players really affected the chemistry we had as a rec team.

We were okay for a club team, winning about half our league games, but we could have done so much better if we had any chemistry, which can make or break a team. Instead, we had cliques, disruptions and too many losses for the talent we had.

I only played club for two years, but the year-round training really helped me develop my skills. Playing against other club teams was always a challenge. The biggest difference between playing on a club team and a rec team is the level of commitment. Most club teams train year round and play in local weekend tournaments. Other club teams travel all over the state for tournaments.

One of the best parts of playing on a club team was our trainer and assistant coach, Michelle Demko. She's a great player from our area who was High School Soccer Player of the Year. She received a college scholarship to play at the University of Maryland.

After college, she played professionally in Germany for a few years, trained with the U.S. National Team and earned an international cap in 1997 against Germany. Later, the season after training our team, she tried out for the newly formed WUSA, was drafted by the Philadelphia Charge and played midfield for them.

It was more fun learning new drills from her than it was from our fathers who served as our coaches over the years. She was closer in age, AND she was a female player.

-2-
Autographs
and Olympic Glory

My interest in soccer led to my interest in the U.S. Women's National Team. One Christmas, I received the 1996 Women's National Team Calendar. I looked at all the player's names, pictures and statistics. Somehow I knew the name Mia Hamm, but that was it. I didn't know any other players.

On February 2, 1996, my parents took Nicole and me to see a double-header match in Tampa between the men's and women's teams from the United States and Norway. I was amazed that the United States Women's National Team, all world-class athletes, was playing against Norway, the 1995 Women's World Cup Champions, and only 2,000 fans showed up. It was raining and there was an overhang for the fans, but the players were getting soaked. The U.S. team won 3-2.

Before the game, my dad said we would not be able to get any players' autographs, because they were the national team and there would be too many people there. So, we left our calendars at home, but we brought our autograph books - just in case.

At the end of the game, we went to a short wall that separated the field from the bleachers, which is where everyone else was gathered. Not only were the players willing to sign autographs, but they even brought their own markers!

Nicole and I got autographs from several players: Mia Hamm, Joy Fawcett, Jen Grubb, Lorrie Fair, Tiffeny Milbrett, Carla Overbeck, Cindy Parlow, Briana Scurry. Two coaches even signed our autograph books - Coach Tony DiCicco and Assistant Coach April Heinrichs.

We stayed for the men's game, and about five minutes into it, the entire Norwegian women's team came up the aisle and sat two rows behind us. After they ate their brown-bag dinners in the bleachers, I asked the player closest to me for her autograph. Not only did she sign my book, but then she passed it to the next player, who passed it to the next, and the next. Well, we ended up with autographs from the entire Norwegian National Team, including international superstars Hege Riise and Marianne Pettersen.

The second game our family saw took place during the opening round of the 1996 Olympics in Orlando. We went with my teammates from the Soccer Maniacs, Alia Tovey and Christie Leak. It was great to see the team play again. They were so strong, so fast and so incredibly skilled. Of course, the U.S. Team won, beating Sweden by a score of 2-1.

After the game ended, our U.S. Team held up a banner that said "Thanks Orlando!" since that's where they were training for the last few months. We thought we had no chance in getting autographs, since there were 28,000 people there. A huge crowd gathered around the exit near where the team buses were parked.

While waiting for the team, we met a man handing out autographed cards of Tiffeny Milbrett - her father. My dad said he must be really proud of everything his daughter has accomplished. He just smiled!!

Mia Hamm on the attack against Sweden.

Photos #1 - 3: Tisha Venturini celebrates her first half goal against Sweden.

**Above: After the game, the team thanks the fans.
Left: Michelle Akers and Kristine Lilly share the thrill of victory.
Right: Michelle responds to chants of "U-S-A...U-S-A!"**

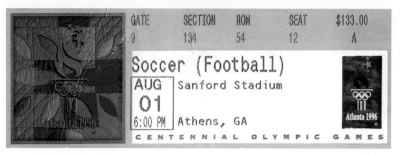

Nicole performs the Macarena, while I enjoy some ice cream between games.

Next, the U.S. advanced to the semifinals against Norway. Because it wasn't televised, my dad called the sports hotline at the *St. Petersburg Times*, our local newspaper, and found out the United States had won. He asked us if we wanted to go to Atlanta for the Gold Medal game, and of course, we yelled "Yes!"

Unfortunately, mom couldn't go because she had to work, but she told my dad to take us on a "Dad and Daughters Weekend!" She's so cool!

So my dad, sister, and I drove up to Atlanta. It took us about 11 hours, but it was well worth it. We arrived about an hour before the Bronze Medal match between Norway and Brazil. After the first game, which Norway won, we walked around the stadium looking for neat Olympic souvenirs. We saw all sorts of t-shirts and pins, but everything was so expensive.

We went back to our seats in time to see the players march onto the field. When they appeared, more than 76,000 fans, the largest crowd for a women's sporting event ever, were screaming "U...S...A!" - " U...S...A!" - "U...S...A!"

The United States was playing China, a team with great ball control, so the ball easily zipped along the grass field. It was an equally played game, until Shannon MacMillan drilled a rebounded shot and scored, taking the U.S. to the lead 1-0. Later, China scored, tying it up 1-1.

In the second half, even though our U.S. Team seemed to be in control, they just couldn't score a goal. Finally, in the 72nd minute, Tiffeny Milbrett scored the winning goal for our U.S. Team. A few minutes later, Mia Hamm went down with an injury. My dad, sister and I started chanting "Mia!" - "Mia!" - "Mia!" Soon, our whole section joined us, but not the entire stadium, which would have been totally awesome.

Above: More than 76,000 fans were on hand to see the Gold Medal game against China.
Below: Free kick in the first half near the box.

When the ref blew the final whistle, everyone was celebrating like crazy! The excitement lasted for the longest time. All the Olympic glory you see on television is even more incredible when you're there - the medals, the national anthem, our flag rising over the stadium.

My dad had brought his camera, so we moved to the endzone of the stadium under the flagpoles, knowing the teams would be facing them, and us, during the national anthem. My dad shot a bunch of photos that night, including one that shows all three medal teams, the bleachers and the scoreboard.

Then the U.S. team paraded around the stadium and later came down right in front of us to be interviewed for television. Everyone from the team looked so happy.

It was easily the best event I had ever seen. Even now, years later, I have a poster on my wall of the U.S. Team after they received their gold medals. I think it's pretty awesome to have a poster of the game I was at! I wonder how many other people who were at the game, have that poster. Probably all of them, except for the Chinese fans.

The next day, we went into Atlanta's Olympic Park and checked out all the Olympic souvenirs. We also saw the women's basketball semifinals with the U.S. Women's Dream Team, but the real reason we went to Atlanta, was for the gold medal soccer game.

Going to the Olympics was one of the best adventures you can imagine. If you ever get the chance to see the Olympics, go for it! It's an experience of a lifetime!

**Top: Celebrating Shannon MacMillan's goal.
Above: Victory lap around the stadium.
Below: Olympic Champions at attention
while our national anthem fills the stadium.**

- 3 -
Calm Before the Storm

After the 1996 Olympics, our National Team didn't play near us for another nine months. Finally, in April of 1997, my grandfather, Papa Big Ed, who was visiting us from New York, took Nicole and me over to the University of Tampa to see our heroes again. Our team was playing against France and beat them 2-1.

After the game, all the players approached the small crowd - there were only about 2,000 spectators - to sign autographs. Once again, they had their own markers, but this time we were better prepared. Soon, my soccer ball was filled with autographs and so was Nicole's shirt. Papa Big Ed caught a photo of the great Michelle Akers signing my ball.

Some of our favorite players - Julie Foudy, Tisha Venturini, Brandi Chastain and Sara Whalen - even posed with us for photos Papa Big Ed shot. Even though they were superstars, they really seemed to enjoy posing with us fans. Nicole and I were so young!

Above: Michelle Akers autographs our ball.
Below: Nicole and I with our heroes: Sara Whalen, Brandi Chastain, Tisha Venturini and Julie Foudy.

Following the Women's National Team back then was often a challenge. Unlike most pro teams, the National Team doesn't have just one home field where they play week after week, for months at a time, year after year. They can play in all fifty states and they'd all be home games for our national team.

Sometimes we could catch them on television, but that too was rare. Besides, it's just so much more fun being at the stadiums, seeing the players in person, and collecting their autographs.

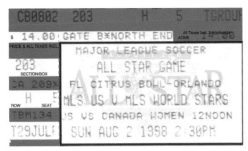

We didn't see them again for more than a year, until August of 1998, when they were scheduled to play against Canada before the MLS All Star Game in Orlando. When my dad was buying the tickets over the phone, the ticket seller told my dad about a special skills clinic to be staged by Michelle Akers. It was scheduled for the day before the Orlando game in Celebration, a city near DisneyWorld.

The man told my dad that the clinic wasn't really publicized because Major League Soccer was staging a clinic of their own with the All-Stars. He said Michelle's clinic was planned mostly to thank the people in the town of Celebration for hosting our team, but it was open to everyone.

I wanted to get something really cool autographed, so I took my ticket stub from the Olympics Gold Medal game and pasted it onto a piece of white cardboard. I noticed the date on the ticket stub, August 1, 1996, and that the clinic happened to be on the two-year anniversary of the Olympic win.

At the clinic, Michelle Akers introduced herself, spoke to the kids, and answered questions, before her demonstration and our clinical work. Michelle then demonstrated Coerver ball skill moves, shooting, passing, and juggling. Her shots were like rockets. She was awesome!

After the clinic, there was a "Meet and Greet" planned where we could get autographs. We spoke with Michelle for a few minutes and she had her Olympic gold medal on display. She was even allowing people to pick it up and wear it. I nervously asked if I could and she said "Yes!"

Imagine, there I was, an eleven year-old kid wearing the Olympic GOLD MEDAL I had seen Michelle win exactly two years earlier. I asked for Michelle's autograph on my special card. Then, I showed her it was the two year anniversary. She yelled to Julie Foudy, "Hey Fouds! Two-year anniversary of the Olympic Gold Medal!"

In addition to Michelle, we also got autographs from Julie, Christie Pearce, Amanda Cromwell, Tracy Ducar, and Debbie Keller. While we were talking to Julie, she asked if we were going to be at the Women's World Cup. We said we might go to the Washington D.C. game. She asked if we were going to the Finals in L.A. I said, "Only if we win some contest."

The players gave us a bunch of stuff: bumper stickers, photo cards, stickers. Michelle even gave us a free copy of her book, "*Standing Fast.*"

The next day, we went to the exhibition game against Canada, followed by the All-Star game. We met up with my teammates Alia Tovey, Christie Leak, and Lindsay Luth-Powell and their families. We watched the U.S. dominate the action right in front of the goal where our seats were.

At halftime, all eighteen of us moved to the opposite end, where the U.S. team was attacking in the second half and found empty seats. We saw mega-action in front of us all day. We cruised 4-0!

- 4 -
Love of Writing

So now you know how much I love soccer. I've played for years and I've been following the National Team for almost as long. But my love of writing opened the door to the most incredible adventure a soccer fan could have.

In the spring of '98, my good friend, Jenelle McKee, was writing her application letter to join the X-Press Team, a special kids' section in the *St. Petersburg Times*, written for kids by kids. Jenelle was trying to make it on to the X-Team. She suggested I should also send a letter.

For me, it was one of those rush-rush-rush-to-get-it-done kind of things. When I asked my parents if I could, they were all for it, encouraging me to send the letter. They also told me that I would really have to sell myself. I finished my first draft, polished it up, and mailed it in:

LEAH LAUBER
6967 Sunset Drive South
S. Pasadena, Florida 33707
(727) 347-4440

Dear X Press,

I would be great for the X-Team because I'm smart, creative, well rounded, a team player, and especially because, I love to write.

I earned straight A's at St. Jude Cathedral School where I also won my class spelling bee. I also did quite well on my Iowa Test of Basic Skills.

I like to draw, make art projects, and make videos with my friends. We made a New Year's Video and then presented it to the people at our New Year's party. I also made a Beanie Baby play with my friends and my sister. We did a modeling show and we started a Beanie Baby Newsletter.

I'm well rounded enjoying playing piano and playing soccer. I love to take photos.

I have a pen pal, and I like to write stories and plays, and I have a summer journal. I wrote a lot of stories about different things like Halloween and Christmas. I even wrote a Lego Story with my friends. I can type 17 words per minute. Also I come from a long line of writers. My great-grandfather was a sports writer for a newspaper. My grandmother was an editor for the Dunedin Times. I have writing in my blood!

My ideas for stories are:
1. A book review, the same thing as the movie review except with books.
2. How to take a photo correctly, like know how to use a zoom and make sure your finger isn't on the flash.
3. Explain what the Soccer Women's World Cup is. Kids might see all this stuff about the Women's World Cup and not even know what it is.
4. Spending a day with the U.S. Women's National Soccer Team.

A deadline I've met is: It was Memorial Day weekend so I only had four days of school that week. For my final grade in school, I had to read a story out of our reading books, then do three pages out of our reading workbook. After that, I had to write a one hundred word essay about the story and then make up a twenty-question test. For spelling, I had to write twenty spelling words five times each and write the definitions.

Being on the X-Team would be a great honor and privilege. I would enjoy it very much and it would be a good experience to see what it is like to work at a newspaper.

From,

Leah Lauber

Leah Lauber

A few weeks later, when the mail came, I saw my name on an envelope from the *St. Petersburg Times*. I tore open the envelope. As soon as I saw the first word, "Congratulations," I started jumping up and down:

St. Petersburg Times

Dear Leah,

Congratulations, the wait is over! You've won a place on our X-clusive X-Team!

The competition was really tough - a lot of X-ceptional kids applied from all over the Tampa Bay area. Please let us know if you choose to accept the X-Team position as soon as possible by calling me, Gretchen Letterman (the X-Press editor), at the number below.

Your first assignment will take you out to the ballgame! The new X-Team will go to Tropicana Field in St. Petersburg of Friday, July 24 to see the Devil Rays play the Oakland A's. You'll be guests of the Times (we'll sit in the Times' box, and supper will be on us) while you meet and get to know your X-Team colleagues.

Of course, you'll also be working! For your first story, we want you to report on the game experience, from the field, to the food, to the funny blue mascot, to the fine or not-so fine souvenirs. You'll get specific assignments the day of the game, along with your X-Press press pass.

We'll send you more details as soon as we have them worked out (such as when to meet at the Times' downtown office to catch the game shuttle bus). You'll need to provide your own transportation to and from the Times that night. To make it easier, we will provide one ticket for your favorite adult to attend the game (located elsewhere in the stands).

If all goes as expected, and you meet your deadlines, you and the other new X-Teamers will be featured on the X-Press page Aug. 3. We have a few other assignments in mind, but we'd like to have your feedback. So, bring along your ideas for future stories to our Tropicana Field meeting.

Through the year you'll be working with me and Pamela Davis (she's the youth culture writer), and we'll both be at the game with you.

Again, we need to know as soon as possible
    (1) if you still want to be an X-Press member;
    (2) if you can come to the first meeting; and
    (3) if your designated driver will need a ticket to the game.

Please contact me by July 13. We look forward to hearing from you!

Sincerely,

Gretchen Letterman

Gretchen Letterman
X-Press editor

I was so excited! I couldn't believe I would be writing for the *St. Petersburg Times*, Florida's largest newspaper, not some little monthly school paper. At our first meeting, we met at the offices at the *St. Petersburg Times* and we were told there were more than one hundred applicants. Just twelve of us were invited to join the X-Team!

Then we went to a Devil Rays baseball game just a few blocks away. We were given a tour of Tropicana Field and, as a group, we met with one of the staff sports writers. He told us about his job, what he likes (watching the games), what he dislikes (the deadlines).

Next, we interviewed one of the players as a group. I asked him three or four questions. It was so cool with our whole group asking him questions and hearing all his responses. I mean, here's a professional athlete, making millions of dollars every year to play his favorite sport, talking to a bunch of kids about his life.

We watched the game from the Times' suite, behind home plate. We enjoyed a great view of the game, and the suite was stocked with food, drinks, cushy chairs and television sets. We were told that Times' employees often entertain special guests in their suite, but that the sports writers watched the game from the press box.

Our first assignment was to write up our thoughts of the game and the questions we asked and the answers we received.

Even though it was a group assignment and each of our comments would be pretty short, I quickly learned how hard it is to write well. First, I would attend an event and/or interview people. Next, I would review my notes, develop an outline, then just type into my computer whatever came into my mind, not worrying about spelling, typing or grammatical mistakes. Then I would go back and edit my article. I would move sentences around, add more information and then carefully polish it two, three, and sometimes four times.

My NanaPat, a writer her whole life for newspapers, magazines and a huge company, taught me to make every word count. This was a lesson she learned from her father, a sports writer and editor for the *Newark Star Ledger* in New Jersey. While my dad isn't a full time writer, he has written many articles and shot thousands of photos which were published. He was even hired back in the day to shoot Spring Break for MTV. So journalism is in my blood. And maybe even a few drops of ink, as well.

During the year, I had some really cool assignments, movie reviews, and concert reviews (Jimmy Buffett and *N SYNC). I also wrote a profile on a schoolmate, Caitlin Stack, who danced in Ireland in the World Championships for Irish Dance.

Above: Each of the X-Press team members were issued an Official X-Press Pass, complete with our photo and signature.

Right: The flip side of our X-Press Pass included the logo from our special section.

Section 2

Meeting MY Dream Team

In THEIR Dream Season

▪ 5 ▪
A Hero Becomes a Friend

Shortly after Danielle Fotopoulos scored the winning goal for the Florida Gators against North Carolina in the NCAA college championship game, I learned she would be coming to my club at Azalea in St. Petersburg to stage a clinic on a Friday night in December of '98.

I thought it would be a great chance to interview Danielle, so I wrote and sent my first "pitch" letter to my editor, Gretchen Letterman. I learned that writers must develop their own ideas for stories, and like everything else, you have to "sell your ideas."

LEAH LAUBER
6967 Sunset Drive South
S. Pasadena, FL 33707
(727) 347-4440

December 14, 1998

Ms. Gretchen Letterman
St. Petersburg Times
via fax

Dear Ms. Letterman,

I'm going to a soccer clinic on Friday which is being held by Danielle Fotopoulos at my club. I was wondering if I could do a story on her. Here are a couple of highlights about her that I think would be interesting for X-Press readers:

1. She is the all time college leading goal scorer with 118 goals.
2. She is on the national team which will be playing in the Women's World Cup next summer in the United States.
3. She scored the winning goal for the University of Florida in the championship game against North Carolina.
4. With the high number of kids playing soccer in this area, it would be interesting for them to read an article about Danielle.

I would like to interview her on Friday. If I can do this story, please call me. Thank you.

From,

Leah Lauber

Leah Lauber

P.S. Jimmy Buffett concert story to follow soon.

Gretchen agreed Danielle would provide an interesting article and asked my dad to shoot some pictures of her and me in action.

Danielle was really nice, especially when I messed up (my tape recorder was on pause and it wouldn't record). She was very patient with me, and that was a good thing, because it was my first time interviewing someone with a tape recorder.

After the interview, my dad needed to shoot the action shot of us for the paper and he said I should juggle the ball with her watching. I was so nervous about juggling in front of a superstar. I didn't know what she would say. Danielle would count out loud for me and was very encouraging. When the ball dropped to the ground, she would tell me to keep trying to see if I could break my record.

My first soccer article described the clinic, and included my interview with Danielle.

Above: Danielle Fotopoulos chatting with players from my club at Azalea.
Below: Danielle demonstrates proper kicking techniques.
Right: Danielle watches as I juggle the ball.
Below right: Some of my teammates and I pose with Danielle and her assistants.

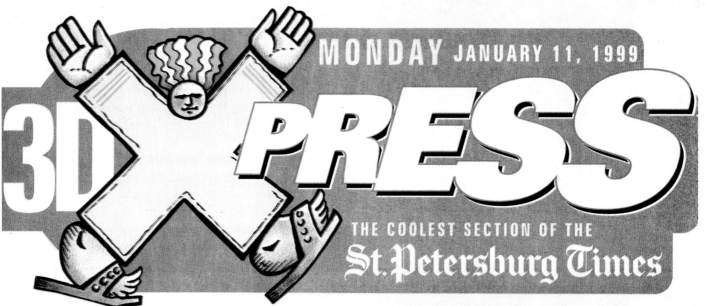

WHAT A KICK!

■ Soccer's leading college goal scorer, also a Women's World Cup contender, offers advice to young players.

By LEAN LAUBER
Times X-Team

There's nothing like getting advice from a pro, and girls in the Azalea Youth Soccer League in St. Petersburg recently had a great opportunity to do just that.

Danielle Fotopoulos, 22, all-time leading college goal scorer for women's soccer and member of the U.S. women's soccer team, conducted a soccer clinic last month for girls of all ages.

In case you didn't know, Danielle will be playing in the Women's World Cup this year, and her record is amazing! She scored the winning goal for the University of Florida Gators in the NCAA championship game against North Carolina last month and was the offensive most valuable player in college. She played youth soccer for the Tampa Town N' Country Heather club, helping her team win the 1995 Athena Cup (under 19) national championship.

At the clinic, Danielle offered many tips about how to become a better soccer player. She ran us through ball control drills, passing the ball and shooting on goal for about an hour.

When we were finished, I got the chance to talk with Danielle.

Leah: How long have you been playing soccer?
Danielle: Since I was 7 or 8.
Leah: What is the most goals you've scored in one game?
Danielle: The most goals I've ever scored is six.
Leah: When did you start getting serious about playing soccer?
Danielle: I would have to say I got serious in my ninth-grade year in high school because I had to choose between soccer and basketball.
Leah: Have you always been a good goal scorer?
Danielle: It's taken me a couple of years to be able to be calm in front of the box (goal). I've always been one to work hard, but definitely being good on the ball is something I need to work on more.
Leah: How often do you practice?
Danielle: I practice two times a day and six days a week. I practice

Photo by CHRIS LAUBER

Danielle Fotopoulos, 22, watches X-Team member Leah Lauber juggle a soccer ball. Danielle posted the winning goal for the University of Florida in the NCAA championship game against North Carolina last month.

Danielle from 3D

in the morning and have games at night; it depends on my schedule.

Leah: Which foot are you better at kicking with?

Danielle: My left foot is stronger and more powerful and my right foot is more my finesse foot, so I kick with both feet, but my left foot is more powerful.

Leah: How many juggles (keeping the ball in the air using your feet, thighs, chest and head) can you do?

Danielle: I think my best is like 215 or something.

Leah: How do you feel about scoring the most goals in college?

Danielle: Just that I'm very thankful for the opportunity that I have been given. I'm thankful for my teammates for getting me the ball because without them, I couldn't have scored those goals.

Leah: What was it like scoring the winning goal in the championship game against North Carolina?

Danielle: It was awesome. You know at the time, I didn't know it would be the winning goal. I was just very glad that we got the ball in the back of the net and we scored before them.

Leah: Have you played with the national team before?

Danielle: Yes, I've been with the national team for about two years.

Leah: What's it like knowing you are going to be playing in the Women's World Cup next year?

Danielle: I'm very excited. I'm happy to say I'll be playing for my country — that's one

accomplishment I've been wanting to do.

Leah: How many soccer clinics have you coached?

Danielle: A lot!

Leah: Do you plan to become a professional coach?

Danielle: Yes, I plan to become a college coach one day.

Leah: What would you recommend is a good workout and how often to do that?

Danielle: I think that depends on the player and the level of the player. You can work on your ball touch and your juggling every day — 15 or 20 minutes of that is something that I worked on my whole life; but also you have to keep up a fitness level. You have to run and sprint a lot. To be a professional athlete, you need to train five or six days a week, a lot of training!

Leah: Why do you think juggling is good for young soccer players?

Danielle: Because it helps you get your touch on the ball; and when you get your touch on the ball, it gives you confidence, something that you need.

Leah: What do you have to say to kids about being successful?

Danielle: Just write down your goals and always put them up on your mirror. Look at them every day and make objectives to meet those goals.

Leah: What do you think is the most fun about playing soccer?

Danielle: I'd say my teammates. I really enjoy my teammates and playing together as a team — that's the most fun about playing soccer.

Leah Lauber, 12, a sixth-grader at St. Jude Cathedral School in St. Petersburg, plays for the Azalea Youth Soccer League.

In January, my story finally came out. When my dad came in my room to wake me up, he had the newspaper in his hands. I hardly had my eyes open (I'm not much of a morning person), but I sat up in bed reading my article. It was so cool to see my first feature article in the *St. Petersburg Times.*

When I finally got out of bed, my mom asked me how I liked my story in print. I thought it looked great, but I noticed the article was edited slightly from what I had submitted - nothing major, but not <u>exactly</u> what I wrote. I learned every writer needs a good editor.

Thank you Danielle!!

- 6 -
Leah Meets Mía . . .
and Joy, Julie, Cindy, Lorrie, Shannon,
Briana and Christie

When we heard that the National Team would be coming to Gainesville in late February of 1999 for a game against Finland, my family was excited and planned to drive up to Gainesville, less than three hours away. But then, we found out it would be on the same weekend as my team's regional club tournament in Winter Haven.

I was really bummed, but there was just no way we would be able to make it from Winter Haven after my own games to Gainesville for the National Team game. Fortunately, a week before the National Team game, it was moved to Tampa, just an hour from Winter Haven. I "pitched" my editor on a few stories, but I knew I really wanted to continue with the soccer stories the most.

LEAH LAUBER
6967 Sunset Drive South
S. Pasadena, Florida 33707
(727) 347-4440

Mrs. Gretchen Letterman
St. Petersburg Times

Dear Mrs. Letterman,

Hi, I have some story ideas for the Express:

1. Caitlin Stack, an eighth grader at St. Jude's, is an Irish dancer. She earned the opportunity to go to Ireland to compete at the World Championships in a few weeks. I was wondering if I could do an article on her.

2. The Women's National Soccer Team is now training in Orlando for the Women's World Cup to be held this summer in the United States. The United States is one of the strongest teams in the world and will have a chance to show how good they are on their home turf.

I would like to volunteer to be the Times Junior Reporter for the Women's World Cup. I would like to write a series of articles leading up to it. During the next 4 months, I could explain what the Women's World Cup is, why kids should be interested, player profiles, a report from training camp, and game reports. For instance, The United States is playing Finland in Tampa on February 27. Even though my soccer team has a game in Winter Haven, I could make it for the second half.

3. 'N Sync is coming to the Ice Palace on May 14th. If nobody has asked, I think it would be good to do a concert review on them.

4. The Harlem Globetrotters are coming to the Bayfront Center on March 9, although I've never seen them play, my dad says they would be great for kids to see.

5. There is a shuttle launch in May at Cape Canaveral, I would like to report what it would be like to see one take off into orbit.

I will be available for the rest of tonight at home; tomorrow from 6 until 7. I'll be available on Wednesday from 3 until 6. Or you could call my dad at his office.

Thank You,

Leah

Leah

Gretchen agreed that attending the National Team's game against Finland would make a good story. She suggested that I should describe the atmosphere, the game and the "scene." It was already the week of the game, so Gretchen suggested I call to make arrangements for press credentials.

Since I was in school all day, my dad called Bryan Chenault from U.S. Soccer for me. I was so excited when he told me I would get a field pass for the game. But the story's focus changed when we were delayed in getting to the National Team game. Instead, I wrote "Soccer Diaries."

Clockwise from top left: Tracy Ducar signs Nicole's mini Women's World Cup ball as my mom thanks her. While Nicole filled up her ball with autographs, I interviewed Mia Hamm, Joy Fawcett, Shannon MacMillan, Julie Foudy, Cindy Parlow, Lorrie Fair, Christie Pearce and Briana Scurry. Check out how many of these players have their own markers in their hands for autographs.

(All interviews appear in full in Section 3.)

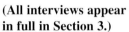

It's a kickin' weekend for one X-team member who lives, eats and breathes soccer for two days.

THE SOCCER DIARIES

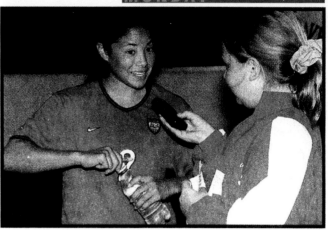

Photo courtesy of LEAH LAUBER

U.S. national team player Lorrie Fair gets interviewed by Leah Lauber of the Times X-Team.

By LEAH LAUBER
Times X-Team Writer

Sometimes you just can't get enough soccer.

Recently, I had one of those times. Here is a journal about my whirlwind whopper soccer weekend:

Friday, Feb. 26, 8:30 p.m.: We are on the road from St. Petersburg to Winter Haven for our regional end-of-season soccer tournament for club teams. It's going to be a fun, but busy, soccer weekend. We have two games tomorrow and one on Sunday.

Overall, we had a pretty good season for a first-year club team. Our league record was six wins, six losses and two ties. We came in fourth in our division out of eight.

After Saturday's games, we will drive back to Tampa for an exhibition game between the U.S. Women's National team and Finland. Our national team is training near Orlando preparing for the Women's World Cup this summer. As a member of the X-Team, I hope to interview some of the players from our national team for future reports on the Women's World Cup.

Friday, Feb. 26, 9 p.m.: We finally arrive at the hotel and while we are getting checked in, my teammates Alia Tovey and Gina Fote arrive right after us. Afterward, we are going to hang out with some of our other teammates, Lauren Vogel and Morgan Bell. It's fun being on a soccer team because you make so many new friends.

Saturday, Feb. 27, 9 a.m.: My team is warming up for the Largo game. Man, they look tough and I know they are. In the beginning of the season, we played them, and the score was 13-0 in their favor. I'm praying that we do well today.

The game starts and we're holding our own when Lindsay Luth-Powell takes a beautiful shot, but their goalie makes a great save.

One of our defenders makes a mistake, and Largo is awarded a penalty kick. Our goalie, Sarah Brady, is moving around on the line. I hope she is making the girl nervous. I'm right! She just kicked it right to Sarah! But Sarah punches it out, and the

girl gets the rebound. She shoots again, but Sarah saves it!

It's half-time, and there is no score. We are all happy. We all know we need to beat Largo to advance to the semi-finals.

Largo scores a goal about 10 minutes into the second half. We slowly fall apart. I can see it happening.

The score ends 3-0 in Largo's favor. We're all

Please see **SOCCER** 4D

pretty upset. We pick up sandwiches at Subway and go to a park to eat lunch. I have a feeling we will do better in the next two games (and I hope we do!).

Saturday, Feb. 27, 2 p.m.: We're ready for our next game against the Tampa Knights, a team we've already beaten twice, but we must wait for the game before us to finish. We start 35 minutes late, which means we are going to be late for the national team game.

Our game just finished. We won 3-0. Rachel Pomeroy scored one goal along with Sarah Brady and Kyla Lemieux. Gina Fote scored, but it was called against us (offsides). My dad went crazy. It was Kathryn Piotti's birthday today and I was hoping she would get a birthday goal, but she didn't.

We immediately leave for Tampa, so I'm still in my uniform and don't have time to change.

Saturday, Feb. 27, 5 p.m.: We just arrived at the University of Tampa for the national game and the score is already 1-0 in favor of USA. Yeah! Mia Hamm just scores another goal (her 104th) for the United States. Good job! I got press passes and arm bands with my dad to go on the field after the game. I'm going to try to interview the players, especially Mia Hamm, the world's best woman soccer player! That would be awesome!

Tweet! The final whistle just blew and hundreds of kids line up to get autographs. I walk on to the field with my tape recorder ready. The first player I see is Danielle Fotopoulos, who I interviewed a few months ago. She saw me and remembered my name. I smiled at my dad because he said she probably wouldn't.

At first I am nervous about interviewing everybody. I walk up to defender Lorrie Fair

and say, "Hi, my name is Leah Lauber. I'm a junior reporter for the *St. Petersburg Times*. Can I ask you a few questions?" She says yes and now I'm cruisin'.

I talk with some other players but can't find Mia Hamm. I look across the field and she is being interviewed by ESPN. When she finishes, I approach her and introduce myself. Now I'm interviewing Mia Hamm! I'm thinking, "Oh, my gosh. I'm interviewing Mia Hamm. This is so cool." Mia isn't all that much taller than me, only about 2 inches. I wake up and see Mia every morning because I have two posters of her in my room.

I finish interviewing Mia and suddenly realize I have talked to almost half of the national team: Lorrie Fair, Brianna Scurry, Julie Foudy, Shannon MacMillan, Christie Pearce, Joy Fawcett, Cindy Parlow and Mia Hamm! I'll use the interviews for future X-Team reports as we approach the Women's World Cup.

As we leave the stadium, my mom buys Mia Hamm jerseys for my sister, Nicole, and me. My dad picks up U.S. Soccer yearbooks for all of my teammates. Before I know it we're on our way back to Winter Haven.

Sunday, Feb. 28, 9:30 a.m.: The wind is howling, which creates a big advantage if it's at your back. Our whole team, especially Christie Leak and Rachel Pomeroy, is playing well against Lakeland, a team we've beaten twice already. Emily Milroy scores our first goal just three minutes into the game.

At half-time, during our huddle, our team is chanting "Cream the corn!" because Lakeland's colors are yellow and green. Emily adds another goal in the second half as does Rachel Pomeroy. Our defense, particularly Ashlee Cooper, Autumn Cooper and Gabby Garcia, is so strong our second-half goalie, Alexis Searfoss, doesn't have to make one save. We win 3-0.

At the end of the game, we all throw water on our coaches to celebrate.

Even though we lost against Largo, we won our last two games; and even though we didn't advance, we still had a ton of fun! I think I'll sleep well tonight!

Leah Lauber, 12, is a sixth-grader at St. Jude Cathedral School in St. Petersburg and plays for the Azalea Youth Soccer League.

7

What it Takes . . .
Hard Work When Nobody's Watching

After meeting so many of the players, I realized they were just regular people. But, I wanted to know what it takes to be a world class athlete. How often do they train? What are their schedules? What sacrifices have they made to become such great soccer players?

I knew a story on their hard work and commitment would be good for the young readers of the X-Press page, so I proposed the idea to my editor, suggesting I watch a training session in Orlando. Gretchen agreed and said I would need the team's permission. She also gave me permission to seek press credentials for any other games, including the Women's World Cup.

Just like the "pitch letters" I wrote to my editor for the other stories, selling her on the ideas for the newspaper, I needed to write a pitch letter to the man in charge of the media credentials, Aaron Heifetz, selling him on my dream to cover the upcoming Women's World Cup.

LEAH LAUBER
St. Petersburg Times X-Press Section
St. Petersburg, FL 33710

March 27, 1999

Mr. Aaron Heifetz
1999 Women's World Cup
2029 Century Park East Suite 1400
Los Angeles, CA 90067

Dear Mr. Heifetz,

I'm a junior reporter for the *St. Petersburg Times* X-Press Pages. I've requested and been approved by my editor, Gretchen Letterman, to file a series of stories leading up to the Women's World Cup. I'd like to spend a day at the training center with the Women's National Team, showing what it takes to become a top athlete. I plan on doing an overview on the Women's World Cup including brief profiles on some of the players. I'd also like to write game reports from the Women's World Cup.

Enclosed are two of my articles, one of Danielle Fotopoulos, and one of my Soccer Diary, which both publicize the National Team and the Women's World Cup.

Could I spend a day at the training center in Orlando, if they come back to Florida? If possible, I could attend during my Easter vacation, which is from April 1 - 11. Also, please consider my request for press credentials for a few of the games. Please send me any press kits along with an application for credentials. Since I'm only twelve, and still in school, my dad will call you sometime next week.

Below is a copy of my press pass. Thank you for your time.

Sincerely,

Leah Lauber

Leah Lauber

cc: Gretchen Letterman

Unfortunately, the mailing address from the Women's World Cup website was incorrect, so when my dad called, Mr. Heifetz had not received my request and had no idea what my dad was talking about. After my dad explained my request, Mr. Heifetz gave my dad the phone number to the training center and said to call him the following week to find out the team's practice schedule.

"WOW! COOL!" I thought. "I'M GONNA' SEE THE TEAM PRACTICE!"

I wanted to thank Bryan Chenault from U.S. Soccer for providing press credentials for the game against Finland and send him copies of my first two stories. I also knew the team would be playing in Orlando against Brazil in May and since I had my editor's approval, I wanted to request press credentials for that game also.

LEAH LAUBER
St. Petersburg Times X-Press Section
St. Petersburg, FL 33710
(727) 347-4440

March 27, 1999

Mr. Bryan Chenault
United States Soccer Federation
1801-1811 S. Prairie Ave.
Chicago, IL 60616

Dear Mr. Chenault,

Thank you for the press credential to the Finland game in Tampa. I didn't get to see the entire game, so I my editor, Gretchen Letterman, suggested I write about on my "all-soccer weekend." Enclosed is my article called "Soccer Diaries".

Also enclosed is an article that I wrote on Danielle Fotopoulos, called "What A Kick" after a clinic she gave at my club. Both publicize the National Team and Women's World Cup.

Please send me a press credential for the May 22nd game in Orlando against Brazil. Since I'm only twelve, my dad will have to chaperone me, so could you please send him a press credential also?

Below is a copy of my press pass. Thank you for your time.

Sincerely,

Leah Lauber

CC: Gretchen Letterman

enclosures

I also sent a letter to Gretchen, my editor, along with copies of the pitch letters, just so she knew what I was doing and wouldn't be surprised if she received a phone call from either Mr. Heifetz or Mr. Chenault.

I really loved going to the games and practices and interviewing the players. Writing the articles was challenging, hard work, but I really enjoyed seeing them in the newspaper. But all these other letters sure were a lot of work, took time to write properly, and weren't nearly as much fun.

Somehow I hoped and believed they would be worth the effort.

LEAH LAUBER
6967 Sunset Drive South
S. Pasadena, Florida 33707
(727) 347-4440

March 28, 1999

Mrs. Gretchen Letterman
St. Petersburg Times
490 First Ave. S.
St. Petersburg, FL 33701

Dear Gretchen,
I am sending you two letters that I have sent to do reports on some of the Women's World Cup games. Here's what I have suggested:

1. Spend a day at the training center
2. Brief profiles on players
3. Go to some of the Women's World Cup

If I will not be allowed to do any of those, please let me know soon.

Thank You,

Leah Lauber

enclosures

One rainy Saturday morning in April, my dad, sister and I drove over to the training center near Orlando to see the team practice and hopefully, interview a few more players. Traffic was heavy, with all the tourists on the roads, and the rain came down real hard a few times. Then we got lost, so when we finally arrived at the fields, there was no one there.

We went into the main building and told the receptionist we were there to see Aaron Heifetz, the team's press officer. The receptionist pointed to a door. When we walked in, there was a big, open room with cubicles along the far wall. Lorrie Fair was sitting at a desk right in front of us talking on the phone. A few other players were standing around a table eating fresh fruit and chatting. There was another big table in the center of the room loaded with autographed posters and balls.

Lorrie asked us if we needed anything and my dad said, "We're looking for Aaron Heifetz." She told us he was in one of the cubicles, but he was talking on the phone. We sat down and waited for him, just watching the players hang out.

While we were waiting, Mia Hamm came out of an office with Coach Tony DiCicco right behind her. He called out to Lorrie, who followed him into the office. Julie Foudy approached us and asked if we wanted some autographs. Of course I wanted her autograph, but instead told her we were waiting to speak with Aaron.

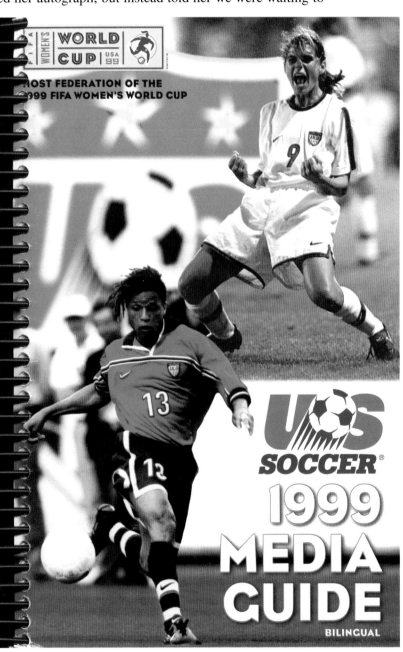

Then Brandi Chastain came up to Nicole, who was pretty big for ten years old, and said "My God! Look at the size of those feet! I was going to give you my cleats, but there's no way you could fit into them!"

She turned around and walked away before any of us could say a thing. We would have taken them off her hands anyway. Who would care if they fit? THEY WERE BRANDI'S CLEATS!

When Aaron got off the phone, my dad introduced us. I interviewed him about the success of the Women's World Cup, ticket sales, television coverage and media requests. He gave me a press kit and an application for media credentials for the Women's World Cup. I then asked him if I could interview some of the players and he said "Sure, just ask them."

I had a real quick interview with Mia Hamm as she was leaving and my dad asked her to autograph the "Soccer Diaries" article, since there was a big picture of her in it. Then I asked to interview Tiffeny Milbrett. She suggested we sit down. After I asked the first question into my tape recorder, she took the recorder from me to answer. When she was finished with her first answer, she put the tape recorder in my face for my next question, like she was interviewing me! It was pretty funny at the time.

I asked Lorrie Fair if she would sign my article "Soccer Diaries," because there's a picture of me interviewing her. She agreed, looked at it, but when she saw the photo, she said "Oh my God! Who took that photo? I look awful!"

My dad just stood there looking upward, and finally said that he had taken the picture. I asked her if I could interview her. She said she was about to get a massage, but that I could interview her during that. So while she had her legs and back worked over by the massage therapist, I interviewed her with my questions about practice and training.

After that, all of the other players had left. Coach Tony DiCicco came out of his office, approached my dad and said to him, "Hi! I'm Tony, coach of the National Team."

My dad said, "Uhh, yeah I know . . . I'm Chris, coach of the Azalea Eagles." Coach Tony just laughed.

I had some questions ready for Coach Tony, but I froze up and he was gone.

Soon, we were driving home, and we listened to the tape recorder. I must have done something wrong with the tape recorder again. I had all the interviews except for Lorrie's. Bummer!

After listening to the tape, I was reading through the media guide and found all sorts of interesting facts about each of the past and current players. There was also a history of the women's national team, including every game they ever played.

Looking at attendance records up to 1999, I learned that I had attended three of the top eight games for all-time largest crowds in U.S. Women's National Team History at home.

Then came the real shocker. For the last two months, my club team was being trained by Michelle Demko, an incredibly good player who I found listed in the pool of national team players. She had told us she had been playing professionally for the last few years in Germany, but never mentioned she had played with the national team. Even though she had only played one game for the National Team against Germany in 1997, I was amazed to see her listed. Just to make it to that level is a real accomplishment.

Even though I didn't get to see the team practice and didn't have enough material for an article on training, it was still a worthwhile trip. It's always great to see and talk to my heroes.

After weather, traffic and getting lost delayed our arrival at the training center, I was not able to complete the article I really wanted to write: what it takes to be a world class athlete. Instead, I wrote a preview article using information from the press kit that Aaron Heifetz gave me, along with some of the quotes I had gathered in Tampa and at the training center.

I included information on how the World Cup would be staged, whose national teams were qualified for the tournament, and some of the more popular websites. The editors included this information as fun facts at the end of my article.

From the time I submitted the article to the time it appeared, seemed like forever, but the editors included it right before the airing of a documentary on Lifetime Channel called "Breaking Through - Women of the World Cup."

Complete interviews appear in Section 3.

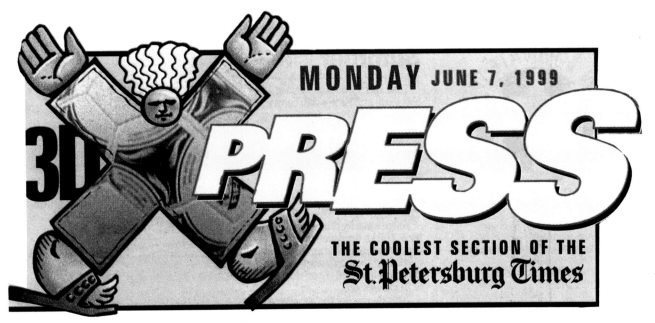

This cup is full of talent

By LEAH LAUBER
Times X-Team

Imagine playing in the biggest sporting event in the history of the world for your gender! Women from 16 countries will have that great experience when they take the field for the 1999 Women's World Cup, the world championship for soccer.

It will be played this summer from June 19 to July 10 in major cities in the United States, including New York, Boston, Los Angeles, Chicago and Washington.

The Women's World Cup is huge, not some small tournament that a few people watch. According to press officer Aaron Heifetz, more than 325,000 tickets have been sold and more than 1,500 press credential applications have been received. That's a lot of reporters and photographers.

All 64 games will be televised on ABC, ESPN or ESPN2.

Why should you care about the Women's World Cup?

"It's soccer's greatest sporting event, and we are trying to make it a breakthrough event, the largest ever in history for women. I think it is going to do a lot, not just for soccer but for women's sports in general," said Mia Hamm, the forward many consider to be the best women's player in the world at an exhibition game in Tampa earlier this year.

"You had the Olympics and that's a huge event, but that's every sport," said forward Cindy Parlow. "The Women's World Cup is just women's soccer and that's it."

The World Cup is "the highest you can reach as a soccer player," midfielder Julie Foudy said.

Goalie Brianna Scurry added, "All women should care about it, and men should care about it because women care about it."

The United States Women's National Team is a great team. In 1998, its record was 22-1-2, losing only to Norway, 1-4. The U.S. team won the Women's World Cup in '91, came in third in '95 and won the '96 Olympics in the first-ever soccer competition in the Olympics for women.

Hamm has scored the most for the United States, with 108 goals, and Michelle Akers has 102. Hamm was also U.S. Soccer's Women Athlete of the Year for five straight years, from 1994 to 1998.

One reason the team is so strong is that its core, including Hamm, Foudy and Akers, has been together for about 10 years, and each knows what her teammate is going to do next. The U.S. team is so good that Danielle Fotopoulos, who set the career scoring record in college with 118 goals, is a substitute.

Although the national team is very good, the competition is also going to be strong. "Norway, China and Germany are always tough, and Brazil has improved over the last four years," said midfielder Brandi Chastain.

"All the teams are going to be dangerous!" said forward Tiffeny Milbrett.

Many national team players think the Women's World Cup will help the growth of soccer, especially since it's in the United States. "You're going to see a lot of girls watching, not just hardcore soccer fans, and, hopefully, an increase in the number of kids playing soccer," Foudy said.

"I think it's the best thing in the world for us to host the biggest women's event in history," said defender Lorrie Fair.

So, watch the Women's World Cup. It will be worth it!

Fun facts to kick around

➤ Sixteen teams, including the United States, Norway, China, Germany and Denmark, competed in qualifying games, playing against teams from the same continent. There are four groups, with four teams in each group.

➤ Each team plays the other teams in its group. The two best teams from each group advance to the quarterfinals and continue single elimination play until the finals, where the champion is decided.

On TV

Breaking Through: Women of the World Cup, 10:30 p.m. Thursday on Lifetime Television.

Soccer on the Web

➤ http://www.wwconthewww.com
➤ http://www.womensoccer.com
➤ http://wwc99.fifa.com/home.html

Leah Lauber, 12, will be in the seventh grade at St. Jude Cathedral School in St. Petersburg.

Soccer Dreams • 27

8

Perseverance Pays Off!

During the spring, it had become much easier to follow the team. They were often on television, and I had found a website called WWContheWWW, which had a message board that I followed. Everyone there had nicknames - mine was Foudopoulos11*17*, my sister's was Brandi6 and my dad's was SoccerManiac. Everyone would post just about anything related to the team, like game reports or getting autographs or opinions on the players.

One guy, Tishoudy, made up a new word for the English language which was related to one of my favorite players, Julie Foudy. "Foudious" was defined as beauteous and graceful while in motion.

There was a lawyer, Tim, who wanted info on how to meet Tisha Venturini. Most of us just told him to get a life!

WWContheWWW went off the internet after the World Cup was over, but all of us refugees found a new home at a message board created by BigSoccer.com.

One day while reading one of my soccer magazines, I saw a short news item about a photo contest sponsored by Hewlett-Packard, the computer company. It was for kids between 12-15, and they wanted a photo of soccer that showed "speed, accuracy, and no compromise."

HP SPONSORS "COLOR IS A KICK" PHOTO CONTEST

Hewlett-Packard (HP), an Official Sponsor of the 1999 FIFA Women's World Cup, has teamed up with the Women's World Cup 1999 to stage a Kick Photo Contest. The competition gives 12 to 15 year olds a chance to win an HP PhotoSmart system, including digital camera and photo-quality printer, and a trip for four to the Women's World Cup final July 10 at the Rose Bowl in Pasadena, California.

To enter, snap your best action soccer shot and tell HP—in 50 words or less— how the photo shows speed, accuracy and no compromises. Send the photo and essay along with your name, age, address, phone number and e-mail (if applicable) by mail to: HP Color is a Kick Contest 11755 Wilshire Blvd., Suite 860, Los Angeles, CA 90025. You can also submit your entry online to the HP Color is a Kick web site at www.hp.com/go/wwc99.

All photos must be the work of the individual contestant. Only one entry per person will be accepted, and the contest ends on May 31. •

Foudious: (fow-de-us) v. 1. beauteous, elegant and graceful while in motion; 2. of or like Julie Foudy; Are You Foudious?

Lucky enough for me, I still wanted to write an article on what it takes to be a world class athlete and we had already made plans to attend another training session in Orlando. Fortunately, I had a day off from school. It would be the last day of residency training in Orlando for the national team.

Even luckier for me at this point, was that Mia Hamm had scored 107 goals, tying her for the international scoring record with Maria Gonzalez, a superstar from Italy. When I last saw the team play in February in Tampa, Mia had scored her 104th career goal for our team.

But after that game, Mia went on an eight-game scoring drought, including the Algarve Cup in Portugal, which the U.S. lost in the finals to China. Back in the United States, Mia's drought continued briefly during a series of "friendlies" called "The Road to Pasadena" which were played around the country to generate interest for the Women's World Cup.

Above, below left: Carla Overbeck and Danielle Fotopoulos practice free kicks.
Right: Carla Overbeck, team captain.
Far right: Lorrie Fair stretches after practice.

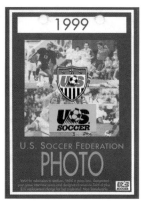

Suddenly, Mia went on a scoring streak with three goals in three games, with the 107th scored the week before I would see the team play against Brazil in Orlando! I hoped I would see her break the record! And I knew I would attend practice the day before that big game.

On May 21, we drove over to Orlando on a beautiful Friday morning in light traffic and we didn't get lost this time. I asked my dad if I could use his camera. He agreed, loaded the camera and adjusted all the settings. All I needed to do was focus and shoot.

I took photos of the team dribbling, shooting, and having a mini-scrimmage. I hoped I would get a good photo for the contest. I knew it would only take one good shot, but I still blasted through two rolls. Action photography is a lot harder than it looks!

After practice, I interviewed Briana Scurry, Brandi Chastain and Danielle Fotopoulos. After I interviewed Danielle, a reporter from the *New York Times*, Jere Longman, approached me and asked to interview me! We talked for a few minutes about me being a fan and a junior reporter. My dad told him that my grandmother clipped his articles for us to read.

Later, while we were driving home, I learned that during practice, Bryan Chenault gave my dad the media credentials for the game the next day, which included two field passes. I screamed, "OMIGOSH - I'LL BE ON THE FIELD FOR THE GAME!!"

My fourth article for the *St. Petersburg Times* described the two-day adventure.

They're on the ball

The Women's World Cup is under way, and the U.S. team worked hard to get there. What does it take to be a world-class soccer player? An X-Team writer kicks that question around.

By LEAH LAUBER
Times X Team

Do you have what it takes to be a world-class athlete? Do you know what it takes? Well, if you don't know, keep reading!

I attended the U.S. Women's National Soccer Team training session at the Seminole Sports Training Center near Orlando recently while the team was preparing for the Women's World Cup, which began Saturday and runs through July 10.

The U.S. Women's National Team is a great team. In 1998, its record was 22-1-2, losing only to Norway. The U.S. team won the Women's World Cup in '91, came in third in '95 and won the '96 gold medal in the first Olympic soccer competition for women.

When we arrived at the field, the team was already warming up and stretching. They were working on individual skills such as juggling, volleys and heading. Then they played small-sided games such as 4 vs. 2, playing to maintain possession of the ball. The purpose was to make the transition to defense as fast as possible once a player lost the ball.

Next, they worked on the fine art of "finishing," or scoring goals. They worked on several ways to attack the goal from different angles.

What impressed me most was that the best women's team in the world was practicing so hard! After practice I spoke to a few of the players.

"We know every other team is playing their best when they face us, so we have to be as good as we can

Please see **SOCCER** 4D

A crowd of reporters, including Times X Team member Leah Lauber, third from left, surround U.S. women's player Mia Hamm.

Lauber family photo

Soccer from 3D

be," said defender Brandi Chastain.

"You have to work hard to stay the best," said goalie Brianna Scurry.

"In order to achieve your goals and get where you want to be, you have to continue to practice," said forward Danielle Fotopoulos. "I always practice year-round with a club team, or doing whatever I can to improve myself."

When the players were younger, they sometimes had to miss parties, dances and sleepovers, just so they could play soccer. Most of us would consider those sacrifices, but they don't; they choose to play for the love of the game.

The rewards are great for these world-class athletes: traveling around the world as a team, getting paid to play and competing in the Olympics.

"That was a dream come true for me," Scurry said about winning the gold medal in the 1996 Olympics.

"I had been dreaming about being in the Olympics since I was really young, so it was an incredible feeling for me. My family was there, my friends were there, we won it at home (in Atlanta), so it was just the most unbelievable experience."

What's the best thing about being on the National Team? "I get to play the sport that I love every day with my best friends," Chastain said.

"The relationships and friendships, we're just a big family here," Scurry said. "I can count on the team for anything."

Though they do take their sport seriously, it's not just work, work, work all the time for this team. During a water break, team members were laughing, joking and throwing water on each other. When the coaches called them to resume, it was instantly back to work. When practice finished, the players still had to attend a team meeting and work out with weights.

"We try to work hard some days, and other days it's easy. It's not hard work every single day. It's a high level of concentration every day, but not physically hard, because we'd just wear the team out," Coach Tony DiCicco said later. "It wouldn't be fun to play, and it's gotta be fun to play."

Of course, the fun part of soccer is playing the game, executing what you've practiced and defeating your opponents.

The next day the team took on Brazil in an exhibition game. I had passes that allowed me to be on the field during the game to shoot photos and to interview the players after the game. (The other photographers there looked at me as if I was just tagging along with my dad, but really, my dad was tagging along with me!)

At that time, Mia Hamm had already tied the record for most international career goals at 107. The players, the media and more than 10,000 fans were expecting her to break the record that night. She had an opportunity to do so early in the game, but the goalie saved it. Right at the end of the first half, Mia shot and scored the record breaking goal. I was standing 15 feet away from her! AWESOME!!! After the referee blew the whistle for halftime, Mia was interviewed by ESPN. As she was going into the locker room, I stuck my hand out and she slapped me a high-five!

During the second half, the U.S. team scored two more goals. The last goal was a set play exactly the way they practiced the day before: one player crossed it from the left side over the goalie to another teammate who headed it back to the middle, where Tiffeny Milbrett converted the easy shot from five yards out. That's what practicing is all about!

After the 3-0 win over Brazil, I was with a pack of reporters and used my tape recorder to capture Mia Hamm's comments about her record-setting 108th goal.

"It was a great ball coming from Cindy Parlow's one-touch pass. She touched it outside because I was running forward. I didn't touch it very well, and I thought I was leaning back, but I guess I hit it right through her legs, so I was lucky this one got through," she said.

"It means a lot to me right now, but it will probably mean even more once I stop playing and look back on my career. I just love the fact that I could be here and share it with my teammates — they're a big part of all these goals," Hamm said. "The fact that they all ran out on the field was awesome. They were telling me how proud they were of me."

She signed my Mia Hamm jersey, as well as my copy of her book, *Go for the Goal*. I also had a binder signed by most of the other players.

Coach DiCicco was sitting on the stairs eating pizza so, between slices, I asked him to sign the binder, too. I laughed when his assistant said, "Here's the head coach of the best women's team in the world, eating pizza on some stairs."

After he finished his late dinner, the coach talked about what makes a national team. "I look for players with character, players that I can trust when we're not together as a team; they're going to work hard even by themselves," he said. "I also look for players that have a special quality. Maybe they're fast, maybe they're leaders, maybe great headers on the ball, but they have to have a special quality. When you get all those qualities together, you can kind of piece the puzzle together."

So now you know what it takes to be a world-class athlete. If you want to become one, get to work!

Leah Lauber, 12, will be in the seventh grade at St. Jude Cathedral School in St. Petersburg.

Mia's complete comments appear in Section 3.

May 22, 1999

USA   **3**

Brazil   **0**

**Top Row: Julie Foudy, Cindy Parlow
Second Row: Kristine Lilly, Kate
Sobrero, Tiffeny Milbrett.
Middle: Mia Hamm
Bottom Row: Michelle Akers,
celebrating Kristine Lilly's goal.**

CONGRATULATIONS
MIA HAMM
A NEW WORLD RECORD
108-108-108-108-108

Top, Red #1 - #7: Mia Hamm and teammates react to Mia's record 108th career goal.
Above, Blue #1 - #3: Minutes later, I high-five Mia on her way to the locker room.
Right: Recording Mia's post-game comments; Mia signing my official jersey.

- 9 -
Dreams DO Come True

The Sunday morning after Mia scored her 108th goal, I had my photos developed from both the practice session and the game. We were sorting through them, but to be honest, most weren't really that good. At least not good enough to enter a national photo contest.

One of my favorite photos from practice was one of the easiest to shoot. The players were carrying the goal into position, so my dad told me to shoot it. At the time, I didn't understand why, but it really shows "Teamwork." Most of the other decent photos were free kicks and pretty easy to get.

Above: Tiffeny Milbrett takes a corner kick right in front of me!
Below: These are my photos of Mia Hamm's celebration after breaking the career record for goals. I wonder why Mia put a move on Julie Foudy to avoid her. Probably just joking around!

I learned how hard it is to shoot good action photography. For instance, Mia was only about 20 feet from me when she scored the record breaker, but I wasn't ready and I missed the shot. But so did my dad, and he's been shooting sports since before I was even born. We both caught a sequence of her celebration though, but mine included Mia dodging around Julie Foudy. I can't believe I have photos of Mia's 108th goal celebration - especially ones that I shot on my own.

One picture from the practice session stood out. It was really good, but the action was kind of small in the frame. So we cropped it and enlarged it into a 5" x 7" print. Much better!

Next, I had to write the essay explaining how the photo showed speed, accuracy, and no compromises. The contest limited us to fifty words, so I had to make every word count. "Speed" and "Accuracy" were easy to include, but "No compromises?" Gimme a break!

Finally, after writing, re-writing, and polishing, I mailed my entry off just before the deadline and began the long wait to see if I was going to the Finals. This is what I sent!

My colorful photo, from an open practice session, shows the importance of running speed, execution speed and accuracy. Playing at full speed, without compromise, this accurate pass splits the defenders.

To prepare for the Women's World Cup, National Team players never compromise at practice. No pain, no gain, no fame.

In the meantime, my parents scheduled a mini-vacation to go to the quarterfinals in Washington, D.C. and then to spend the Fourth of July in our nation's capitol with my cousins. I was also waiting for a response from the Women's World Cup press office to see if I had media credentials for the Washington quarterfinals. Finally, I got permission. WOW!! I'll be able to interview some of the players after a game in the Women's World Cup.

Even though I was excited about the press credentials, I was kind of disappointed that I hadn't heard anything from Hewlett-Packard yet. Every day, I would check the snail mail, my e-mail and our answering machine to see if I had won. Nothing!

My reaction to the phone call learning I had won the photo contest, "WE'RE GOING TO LOS ANGELES!!"

On Friday, June 25, just two weeks before the Women's World Cup Finals, I came home at 5:30 p.m. from my NanaPat's house. My dad was working on the computer. I asked, "Any mail?" No! "Any phone calls?" No! He explained that it was almost 3:00 p.m. in Los Angeles, contest headquarters, and that if we didn't hear by 8:00 p.m., our local time, that I probably didn't win. I was so bummed out, I just went into my room. I really thought I had a photo and essay good enough to win.

I was having some friends sleep over that night. My friend Kelly arrived and we were just hanging out waiting for our other friends. Right at 6:00 p.m., the phone rang and my dad said, "Leah, this may be your winning call." I hurried to pick up my phone, but I couldn't find the portable. My dad had already answered and was talking to somebody.

I picked up my phone and listened in. I heard "...your travel arrangements..." so I hung up, thinking it was USAirways calling about our flight to Washington, D.C. Then, my dad yelled out, "Leah, come here! You have a phone call."

I went into the kitchen and took the phone from my dad, who had his camera in his other hand. A lady on the other line said, "Leah?"

All I said was "Yeah!" My dad started snapping pictures of me.

"Hi. My name is Jules Andres from Hewlett-Packard."

"Yeah?"

"Congratulations! You've won our photo contest! You're coming to L.A."

"YAHOOOO!!!" I screamed. "WE'RE GOING TO L.A."

I started jumping up and down. Kelly came into the kitchen, and I screamed to her "I'M GOING TO THE FINALS!!" I couldn't believe I would see our team in the Women's World Cup Finals . . . IF they won the rest of their games. "No problem," I thought. But in sports, there are always opponents who want to win just as badly. There is always the possibility of losing. Anything can happen during any game, but that's why they play the game . . . and that's why we watch!

- 10 -
One Dream Turns to Nightmare . . .
. . . With a Happy Ending

Our trip to the World Cup Quarterfinals was supposed to be a dream come true. I had media credentials to interview the U.S. Women's National Team after the game and we had great seats. That day I learned dreams can turn into nightmare. My trip to Washington D.C. was a nightmare.

As we were getting ready to leave for the airport, we got a phone call from USAirways, the airline we were flying on. I answered the phone and the lady on the other line asked for my mom or dad. I gave the phone to my dad and just watched him talking. After a few seconds, he said, "But we've got to get to Washington!" I knew that couldn't be good.

After a few more minutes, my dad finally said, "Our flight's been cancelled, but we can get on another one." He told us the times of the flights and chose one that was only 15 minutes later than our scheduled flight. We figured that was okay, but the only bad part was that we had to wait in line for the tickets.

When we arrived at the airport, the line was huge. We waited for about an hour and finally when we got up to the counter, the customer rep typed in our name. Finally, he said there weren't any tickets for us. The lady on the phone never typed our name in. So the rep said he could put us on stand-by for a flight to Philadelphia, then we could back-track to Washington. He also said the chances of us all getting on the same plane were pretty unlikely.

We waited for another hour, while they loaded everyone on the plane. The gate attendant started calling people for stand-by. But they only had two tickets for us. All four of us were really upset. My dad and I went on that flight. I cried all the way to Philadelphia, because I didn't know how my mom and Nicole would get to Washington. That flight was awful.

When we arrived in Philadelphia, my dad said to stand in line while he made a call on a payphone to figure out where my mom and Nicole were. He told me that if I got to the counter before he was back, to just say, "Lauber - two tickets to Washington D.C., together please."

So when I got up to the counter, I did just that. The lady typed in our name and said, "We don't have you listed." I thought "Perfect. Now we're stuck in Philadelphia." I motioned to my dad and when he came over, the lady had found our tickets. We were relieved, but then had to run through the terminal to catch our plane. It was so small, I had both the aisle seat and the window seat. There were only two seats to a row with an aisle down the middle. There were only nineteen seats total and you could look right into the cockpit and see the pilots.

I slept most of the way, but when I woke up, we were going around in circles. This went on forever. We finally landed, but then had to go to a totally different terminal. It took us a while to get our luggage and our rental car.

We were told that Jack Kent Cook Stadium was all the way on the other side of the city and it would take an hour to get there. The game was at 7:00 p.m. and it was already 6:00 p.m., plus it was rush hour. Of course, we got lost and then we ended up in downtown Washington.

```
JKC0701   104       21  21      ADULT
EVENT CODE        SECTION/AISLE  ROW/BOX  SEAT
   75.00   A - LOWER              75.00
          PRICE
    7.25      WOMEN'S WORLD CUP  USA 99
   104              EVENT 14
SECTION/AISLE
AM  83X        DOUBLEHEADER
   21  21     QUARTER FINALS
ROW/BOX  SEAT
603AWWC   JACK KENT COOKE STADIUM
29JUN99 THUR JULY 1, 1999 7:00 P
```

38 • Soccer Dreams

We were stuck at a red light, with the Washington Monument on the right and the White House on the left. Suddenly, there was a big motorcade and a bunch of big, black cars. I asked my dad if it could be the president, and he said, "No, there would be the little flags on the hood of the cars."

I figured he was right, I mean, what are the odds? We were going in the same direction as they were, so we stayed behind them. Then we saw traffic stopped so the motorcade could go through. My dad said, "Hey, I think that IS the president - maybe he's going to the game."

We started following them, but then my dad said "What if Bill is taking Hillary out to some French restaurant? Wouldn't we look stupid if we followed them?" So, he decided not to follow the motorcade and we took a different route.

After awhile, we stopped at a Wendy's because we had to go to the bathroom and we had to ask for directions. When I walked in, I got a lot of stares, probably because my whole face was painted as an American flag.

The lady behind the counter said the stadium was right behind Wendy's. Finally, after twelve hours of travel, we made it to the stadium.

When we were walking to get our tickets at the "Will Call" booth, we could see through the stadium to the scoreboard at the opposite end. It was halftime and the score was 2-1 in favor of Germany. I said, "This can't be good." and kept walking towards the "Will Call" window.

Right: Mia Hamm on the attack in the second half against Germany.
Below: Tiffeny Milbrett controls the ball, while surrounded by the German defense, as Julie Foudy provides support.

Once we had our tickets, I asked where I could pick up my media credentials. They pointed us in the wrong direction, so we just went to our seats, because we were so anxious to see some soccer.

As we were walking through the tunnel, we heard a loud roar from the crowd. Brandi Chastain scored, tying up the game 2-2. The U.S. was back even. Hey, maybe my dad and I brought them some good luck (yeah, sure, in my dreams!).

Even better, my mom and sister were already in their seats. They beat us to Washington and to the stadium!!

We settled in, found out Brandi scored an own goal, and starting watching the game. Shortly after, we looked up at the Big Screen and who's up there, but President Clinton and his family. We should have followed him, because he really was on his way to the game!

Soon, there was a substitution and Shannon MacMillan ran in to take the corner kick. On her first touch on the ball, she kicked a perfect line-drive and Joy Fawcett headed it right into the goal. The U.S. was in the lead! We held on to win the game 3-2 and move on to the semifinals.

Above: Kristine Lilly in the open.
Below: Joy Fawcett's game winning header off Shannon MacMillan's corner kick.

The scoreboard says it all!

The entire United States team celebrated at midfield, before taking a victory lap around the stadium while the German players showed their disappointment.

After the game, before the Nigeria-Brazil match, we once again tried to find my media pass so I could go interview the players, but nobody knew where we should go. Eventually we found the press office, but unfortunately, by the time I arrived in the interview area, nearly the whole team bus was loaded.

I did catch Tiffeny Milbrett for a real quick interview as she walked to the bus:

U.S.A. celebrates and leaves another opponent on its back.

Leah: Did you feel any pressure when you were down one goal?
Tiffeny: No. We felt more mad at ourselves because we let Germany get the goal because of our mistake.
Leah: Were you ever overwhelmed by the number of people in the stadium?
Tiffeny: No. I think it happened in just the first game when we came out and we were in awe over how many people there were in the stadium. But after that, no.

Most importantly, I had a press credential for the Women's World Cup, which I hoped I could use at the Finals.

Even though it was a nightmare of a day for my family, and come to think of it, for the U.S. National Team as well, it ended up just fine. A dream-come-true became a nightmare with a happy ending.

The traditional victory lap.

- 11 -
Dream Becomes Reality

Considering I just experienced one of the worst trips of my life, I was really looking forward to our journey to Los Angeles. The cab driver picked us up early in the morning and we were at the airport with plenty of time before the plane left. Delta Airlines boarded us on-time, and everything went smooth during the long, cross-country flight. What a difference!!

When we arrived in L.A., there was a young man holding up an adidas - Women's World Cup sign, so we approached him. He helped us with our suitcases and took us outside for a shuttle to our hotel. We were the only ones on the bus, so we spread out. En route to the hotel, we saw an adidas billboard, where there was a little naked baby chasing a soccer ball. We saw Women's World Cup banners everywhere. L.A. was definitely ready for the World Cup.

When we arrived at the Hyatt, the lobby was decked out with banners and signs welcoming everyone to the Women's World Cup. Our rooms weren't ready since we were there so early.

We went upstairs to the adidas Hospitality Suite. The women from adidas gave my parents, my sister, and me four Women's World Cup bookbags loaded with shirts, pins, and other stuff, along with name badges to wear in the Hospitality Suite. As a co-sponsor of the photo contest, adidas also gave my dad an envelope with $160 in it for us to use for lunch the next day. We hung out in the Hospitality Suite until our room was ready, watching videos and talking with some other adidas guests.

Hewlett-Packard had reserved two rooms for us - a regular one and a two-room suite. The "regular" room was huge, with two full sized beds and a balcony with a great view. There was even a phone next to the toilet. The two-room suite was even nicer, with a living room and a bedroom, two televisions, two phones, a small refrigerator and once again a phone in the bathroom. There was a shower and a separate bathtub. First class all the way!

We were headed back down to the Hospitality Suite to check on plans for the rest of the day, when a bellhop came walking towards us. He had four duffel bags with the Women's World Cup logo on them. They were for us, from Hewlett-Packard, with more shirts, a water bottle, and another pin. I thought, "This just keeps getting better!"

Our hosts from adidas loaded us on buses for a trip to UCLA for the "Soccer Lab," a series of fun soccer activities, like shooting and dribbling contests. There was a small celebrity scrimmage taking place and we had our pictures taken with a Hewlett-Packard digital camera in front of different backgrounds. Then their color printer printed them out in seconds. Very cool!

Later, back at the Hyatt, we walked over to the hotel next door, which was the FIFA headquarters. Their annual convention was taking place and we saw people from many different countries and cultures. Soccer truly is the world's most popular sport.

That night, we took a bus to Universal Studios, which was much larger than the one I had been to in Florida. We went on a guided tour around the backlot, where sets from famous movies still stood. The tour allowed us to experience flash floods, an earthquake, and a bridge falling apart. We entered the volcano from Dante's Peak, which started "spinning," so when we came out, I felt like I just got out of the dryer. There was also a set from Jaws, where a fake man gets pulled under the water by a giant shark.

After the tour, Hewlett Packard and adidas set up a huge, buffet dinner for us guests, with several kinds of pastas, a roast, breadsticks, and the biggest dessert table I ever saw. We briefly met some real neat people - Cindy Parlow's parents were there as guests of adidas, along with the owners of Eurosport, the giant catalog company.

We were exhausted from all the activities combined with jet lag from the early flight, so we took the first bus back to the Hyatt. What a great first day in L.A.! I slept well that night.

On Friday morning, my family drove out to Pasadena in a rental car provided by Hewlett-Packard. Since practice was closed to the public, Nicole and my mom decided to check out the city while my dad and I went to the Rose Bowl.

When we arrived, practice had just finished, but I was there mainly to interview the players. They were all hanging out on the field, some were stretching, some were just joking around, others were signing autographs for the handful of fans who made their way into the stadium.

Joy Fawcett was one of the players signing autographs, so I made my way to the front of the crowd. I asked her to sign a large picture that my dad shot of her winning goal in the Quarterfinals against Germany. She just signed the photo without really looking at it and moved onto her next autograph.

Then I gave Joy another photo and said it was hers to keep. Once again, she didn't really look at it until she had finished with the autographs. She first looked at the photo when she went over to the bench, and a big smile came to her face. Some of her teammates looked over her shoulder and they were all glad to see the photo. My dad felt so proud.

A few minutes later, a few hundred reporters were allowed on the field, but only to follow the team into the locker room for interviews. When I approached Danielle Fotopoulos, she looked at me and said "Leah, what are YOU doing here?" I explained that I won the photo contest and showed her a copy of the photo, which I asked her to autograph for me, since she's in it. I also hoped to get that print signed by Michelle Akers, Shannon MacMillan, and Kate Sobrero, since they are also in the photo.

Using my press pass, I entered the locker room, which was mobbed by reporters, to interview some of the players. Most of the time, I just hung out, recording the comments from the players, while the "professional" journalists from all over the world asked the questions.

What a blast I had, just bouncing from one player to the next, listening to them speak, recording their comments and asking a few questions of my own. I really wanted to make sure I spoke with some of the players I had never interviewed, like Kristine Lilly and Michelle Akers. I was also able to get Kate Sobrero and Shannon MacMillan to sign my photo.

When my dad gave Shannon a photo of Joy's winning goal, her face lit up and she said, "Cool, when I saw Joy's copy, I wanted one!" Of course, it was Shannon's corner kick that set up Joy's goal, and you can see her in the background watching the goal being scored. A few minutes later, Shannon was nearly the last to board the bus. We could see her passing the photo around to her teammates. What a great way to spend some time, interviewing my heroes.

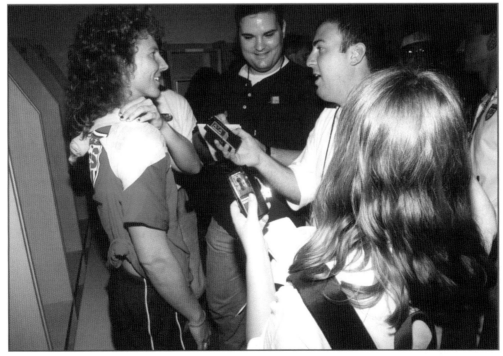

Michelle Akers ices down her injured shoulder, while being interviewed.
All locker room comments appear in Section 3.

After the bus left, we went outside the stadium into the media center, where a bunch of Hewlett-Packard computers were set up with journalists from around the world working on their stories. Other people were just hanging out, chatting. There were also several tables loaded with press releases and media guides. My dad and I took one of each.

Then we went into the center of Pasadena to meet up with my mom and Nicole. The city was preparing for a giant pre-game rally with a concert on Main Street. Everywhere we went, it seemed that everyone was buzzing with excitement. We didn't stick around though, because Hewlett-Packard had arranged for other entertainment for us that night.

On the way back to our hotel, we stopped at a store to buy poster boards, magic markers and face point. We needed to be prepared for the big day!

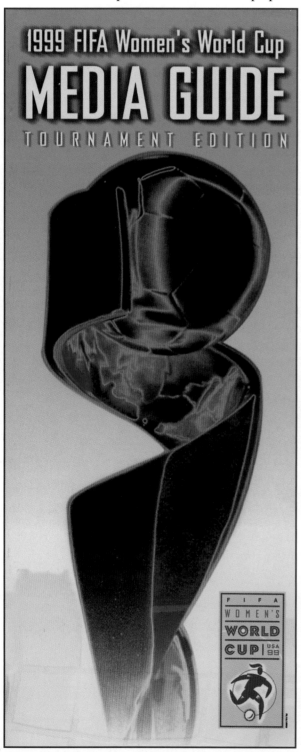

That night, we went to the Hollywood Museum for dinner and a party sponsored by adidas. Once again, there was a huge buffet and the place was decorated to the max with Women's World Cup stuff. We walked around the museum and saw props, costumes, and sets from television shows, including the complete set from the classic show, "Cheers." My parents really enjoyed that since they once lived in Boston, where the show was set, and watched the show all the time.

In a screening room with about a hundred seats, there was a continuous movie playing showing Joy Fawcett, Shannon MacMillan, and Kristine Lilly being interviewed while teaching kids at a camp. It was real cool hearing their stories and watching them teach little kids how to play soccer. Since it was so loud everywhere else, we stayed in there for most of the time.

I finally met Jules Andres, the woman representing Hewlett-Packard, who had called me to tell me my photo won two weeks earlier. Later, Run DMC was scheduled to perform, but they weren't going to start for awhile, so we didn't stay to see them.

We caught the first bus back to the Hyatt, but this time, instead of going to bed right away, we made posters for the big game. My mom couldn't stand the smell of the markers, so she went to sleep while my dad, sister and I worked on the posters in the suite.

I made a poster with a big, red heart that said in the middle "Tampa Bay Loves Danielle!!" and another one that said "Foudious (adj.) - of or like Julie Foudy. Thanks Tishoudy!" My dad made one that said "Real Men Love Women's Soccer!" My sister Nicole made one that said "Awesome Brandi Chastain" for ABC, which was broadcasting the game.

We were also watching The Late Show with David Letterman on television because he had a repeat of a show with Brandi Chastain on it. After it was over, I went back to my room pretty late, but that was okay, because I'm a night owl, not a morning person.

Of course, I can make exceptions. Especially for the Women's World Cup Finals!

My mom, Nicole and I suited up for the big game. My club team's uniform was perfect to show who I wanted to win.

I woke up the next morning really excited. Finally, July 10th, the Women's World Cup Finals would be played in just a few more hours. After some juice in the courtyard of the Hyatt, we went back to our rooms to get ready. I put on my soccer jersey from my club team, which was so All-American: a red-white-and-blue flag design with a giant eagle on it. Then I went through my checklist: tape-recorder, blank tapes, batteries, camera, film, face paint, sunscreen, shades, hat, posters. Yup, I was ready!

We took a bus to the Twin Palms restaurant in Pasadena for a special brunch to recognize the four winners of the photo contest. On the bus, each of the winners were given the Hewlett-Packard digital cameras we had won. After some quick instructions, we started playing with our new toy. It was really neat, because we would take pictures and then look at them right on the camera. I don't know about the other winners, but I erased all of my practice pictures, because I wanted to use the camera for game photos.

When we arrived, there were posters set-up to show each winner's photo and essay. Next to each poster, there was a computer with our winning photo on the monitor, along with pictures of each kid. The three other kids had school photos, but since my dad took my photo of when I won, that was the photo they used on mine. Next to the computer was a color laser printer, which printed out copy after copy of the design on the screen.

At the photo contest winner's reception, Hewlett-Packard had a computer and color printer set-up for each winner, with color prints being produced non-stop, along with posters of our winning photos.

We had our pictures taken next to the display and there were cameramen shooting video of us hanging out with our posters. We also met several Hewlett-Packard employees, who were all very nice. Their photographer even gave me a Women's World Cup Media pin, which are real hard to get, because of my position with the *St. Petersburg Times*.

After brunch, we took the bus to the Rose Bowl for the game. We were given our tickets, which were huge and looked beautiful. I figured the seats must be great, since Hewlett-Packard was such a big sponsor of the tournament. Then my mom put the face paint on me and Nicole. I had a blue star with red and white stripes coming out of it, like the American flag, on my right cheek, with three stars - one red, one white, and one blue on my left cheek. I also had "USA" written on my forehead.

Leah Lauber
12 years old
St. Petersburg, Florida
Grand Prize
Southeast Region

Color **is** a Kick!
Photo Contest

Above: Hewlett-Packard color copy.
Left: Hewlett-Packard press release announcing the photo contest winners.

With my game face, I am sooooo ready!

Enter
GATE   SEC   ROW   SEAT
F   17   5   103

Saturday, July 10,1999

Rose Bowl

10:30 a.m. Kickoff

USA 99   EVENT 17

Third Place Game
Ceremony/Final Game

$110.00   Category I
Rose Bowl, Los Angeles

THIS IS MY GAME

F I F A
WOMEN'S
WORLD
CUP | USA 99

WATCH ME PLAY

Left: The most beautiful ticket I've ever seen!
Above: Tickets in hand in front of the Rose Bowl!

The Hewlett-Packard / adidas Soccer Lab was set up and loaded with kids, but instead, each of us winners was interviewed so the public relations department could send video to our hometown television stations and to CNN. I was first up and I was pretty nervous with this huge video camera stuck in my face. I just tried to answer the questions as best as I could without stumbling over the words.

All the Hewlett-Packard photo contest winners were interviewed before the game.

Right: Our National Team realized their dream of playing in a packed stadium for the 1999 Women's World Cup Championship.

Below: Our seats were great - about ten rows from the field.

Before going into the stadium, we took pictures in front of the Rose Bowl, with me holding the tickets and my sister next to me. We went inside the Rose Bowl and we saw where our seats were - about ten rows behind the U.S. bench. Unbelievable!!

We missed the consolation game between Brazil and Norway because of the brunch and the interviews. We arrived at our seats just in time to see the penalty kicks, which Brazil won. Before the Finals, my mom took my sister and me to get an ice-cream because it was so hot. While we were eating it, we heard these jets go right over the Rose Bowl. We asked someone what time the game started, and they said 1:00 p.m. so we hurried back to our seats.

The atmosphere was totally festive. The stadium was covered with huge banners for the Women's World Cup. Everywhere we went, we saw the Women's World Cup logo. There were fans covered in face paint, most

Standing at attention for our National Anthem, ready to make history.

Above: Brandi Chastain
Below: Team Captain Carla Overbeck

as an American flag. People had their hair dyed red, white, and blue. It seemed like everyone either wore Mia Hamm jerseys, white shirts with an American flag, or for guys, no shirt with "USA" written on their chest. Everybody was so excited. It seemed like we all knew we were about to witness sports history!!

There were also many Chinese fans at the stadium. They had on all red, and a Chinese flag with them, but I didn't notice those, I was looking mostly at the USA fans and banners.

Before the game started, I recognized George Fotopoulos, Danielle's husband, from a clinic I attended in Tampa during the winter. He was sitting in the row behind us, about five seats away. I told my dad. He said to hold up my "Tampa Bay Loves Danielle" poster. I did, and my dad screamed out "Hey, George!" He looked over and saw my poster. George smiled, gave me a thumbs-up, and took out his camera. He took my picture, so now I might be in Danielle's scrapbook holding up my poster!!

Once the game started, both teams were playing very well and you could tell it would be a battle to the finish. Every minute was so intense, because each team's defense was so solid. It seemed like one mistake could mean the difference in the game.

Left: Michelle Akers in control in midfield.

Right: Akers and China goalkeeper Gao Hong battle for a high ball in the box.

Brandi Chastain battles for a headball on a corner kick, while Kristine Lilly, Tiffeny Milbrett and Briana Scurry protect the goal. Lilly would later make the save of a lifetime from her position on the near post.

Kristine Lilly avoids the China defense.

At halftime, Danielle was kicking the ball with a teammate and the ball went right in front of us. As she ran in our direction, my dad yelled out "Danielle!!" When she looked up to see who was calling her, I was holding up my poster. She looked up, read my poster, smiled and waved. I was so glad I made it for her, it was worth the effort!

The second half was even more intense than the first. Since there was no score, everyone knew it all came down to this half. The action went back and forth with both teams trying their hardest to score a single goal, but neither team did.

Since nobody scored, they would play two sudden death overtimes, meaning the first "golden goal" would win the 1999 Championship. Bad news. Michelle Akers, who went down hard in a collision in front of the goal at the very end of the game, had to miss the overtime.

Julie Foudy in wide open space.

Michelle Akers gets nailed in this battle for the ball on a corner kick, forcing her to leave the game.

Above: Carla Overbeck scores on her penalty kick.
Below: Joy Fawcett is congratulated after scoring.

Kristine Lilly made the save of her life, when a head ball came right at her on the goal line after a corner kick. She saved the goal, then Brandi Chastain cleared the loose ball from the penalty box!

When nobody scored in those overtimes, the game went into penalty kicks. Both teams had five penalty kicks. The first two for each team, both teams scored. But, on the third kick for China, goalkeeper Briana Scurry made a great diving save. Everyone in the stadium went wild except the Chinese fans. On the next kick for the United States, Kristine Lilly scored, giving us a 3-2 lead.

In the next round, China scored, but so did the United States to maintain the lead, 4-3. On the next kick, China had to score to stay alive and they did, to tie it up. On the United States' fifth kick, Brandi Chastain walked up to the ball, placed it carefully, then settled down to take the shot seen around the world. She ripped a lefty into the top right corner of the goal and scored the winning goal, 5-4. Brandi ripped off her shirt and swung it around, then fell to her knees screaming. The U.S. were the World Champions!! The stadium erupted in cheers.

Brandi's teammates came running towards her and she was toppled by them. The best celebration began, with wild cheering, music, flags waving. Everywhere you looked, it was just a huge party scene.

Left: Briana Scurry makes the save of a lifetime!
Bottom left: Kristine Lilly after scoring.
Bottom middle: Mia scores the 4th penalty kick.
Bottom right: Mia congratulated by her teammates.

In this sequence, the U.S.A. team reacts with joy to Brandi Chastain's winning penalty kick, and sprints down the field, where Brandi is already celebrating. In the background of the bottom photo, Briana Scurry celebrates as well.

"WE ARE . . .

THE CHAMPIONS . . .

At one point, Briana Scurry came up to our section, and started up our aisle to see and hug her best friend. Michelle Akers emerged from the locker room to a thunderous ovation from the fans. We later learned that she watched the overtimes and penalty kicks with IV's hooked up to her to replenish the fluids in her body.

Then, the players received their medals. First, the Chinese team got their silver medals. When the U.S. received their gold medals, they started jumping up and down, celebrating. Confetti came shooting out of these cannon-type things and showered the players. Everyone was cheering, soaking up the moment. Everywhere I looked, I saw celebration!

The players from the 1991 World Cup Championship team, wearing their own U.S. jerseys, walked down our aisle towards the field, but the guards wouldn't let them on the field. Everyone in our area started chanting "Let them on! . . . Let them on!"

Eventually, the guard let them on and the 1991 World Cup team celebrated along with the 1999 World Cup team. Someone had given all the players bright yellow shirts with 1999 Women's World Champions across the chest and they all put them on. Soon, the players ran a parade lap around the field, waving, smiling and enjoying the best moment of their careers.

Finally, the players made their way to the locker rooms and the fans started to leave. I, too, left the Rose Bowl, but my dad and I worked our way around to the press tent.

OF THE WORLD!!"

Above: The Champions are showered in confetti.
Below: One last victory lap for the Champions.

Above: The scoreboard says it all.
Below: Danielle Fotopoulos with the World Cup.

The 1999 Champions, led by Brandi Chastain, embrace players from the 1991 World Cup Champion team.

I had my press pass, so I was able to go inside to interview the players. It was so cool! I just showed the guard my press credential, and I was allowed in. Bryan Chenault from U.S. Soccer allowed my dad in also to keep an eye on me. I was the youngest journalist, by far, under the tent.

At first, Briana Scurry, Brandi Chastain, and Coach Tony DiCicco were up on a stage answering questions in front of hundreds of journalists. I walked in on that, and held my tape recorder up to the speaker next to me so I could get their comments. Next a few Chinese players and their coach were on the stage for their questions. They didn't look too happy!

Then, Tiffeny Milbrett, Shannon MacMillan, and Mia Hamm were up on the stage, but by then, several of the U.S. players were spread out around the tent for individual interviews. I recorded quotes from Tiffeny and shot pictures of her with my digital camera. I also took pictures of Shannon MacMillan and Mia Hamm talking to reporters.

Next, I went over to Briana Scurry to get some quotes from her. Kate Sobrero was close to her, so I got quotes from Kate also. There was a huge crowd of reporters around Brandi so I chose not to go near her. Then, I walked across the room, to the middle, where I got quotes from Marla Messing, Executive Director of the FIFA Women's World Cup.

Julie Foudy was nearby, so I was able to get some good quotes from her, before she had to go to the bathroom. Kristine Lilly, holding Joy Fawcett's daughter, Kate, in her arms, described her game-saving head ball, "I would have looked pretty stupid if I missed it - I mean it came right at me!. . ." When Julie came back, I went over to her for more quotes, but the batteries on my digital camera needed to be re-charged, and my tape recorder had no tape left, so it was time to leave. That was the greatest time, seeing my heroes enjoy the highlights of their careers.

We took a shuttle bus back to the center of Pasadena to meet up with my mom, Nicole and the rest of the Hewlett-Packard people at the Twin Palms restaurant. When we got off the shuttle bus, there was someone selling copies of the local paper - a souvenir edition with the headline announcing the

Above: Heroes Briana Scurry and Brandi Chastain in the press tent after the game.
Below: Tiffeny Milbrett on stage.

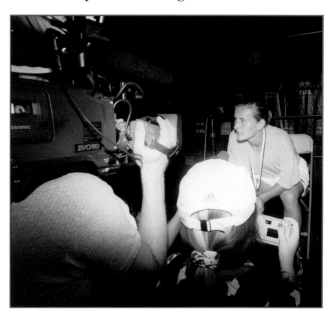

U.S. victory.

As we walked to the restaurant, people in cars were screaming and hollering down the road. "Wahoo! USA won!" The party continued into down-town Pasadena.

At the restaurant, there was dinner waiting for us. Some people came up to me and asked if I was one of the contest winners. I answered "Yes." Press releases had information on the contest, including a short paragraph about me, saying I was a junior reporter for the *St. Petersburg Times*. That was really cool because so many people read the press releases.

Back at the hotel, the Hospitality Suite was open and we went in there just to hang out. On the news, there was non-stop coverage of the women winning the World Cup. We turned it up really loud. A woman from adidas gave us great looking t-shirts that said "USA Champions" on them, along with other soccer shirts with USA on them. They were awesome.

That was the greatest day of my life!

An exhausted, but very happy, Mia Hamm after the game.

- 12 -
A Taste of Victory

During halftime of the big game, my dad said there was going to be a rally for the U.S. Team on Sunday, whether the team won or not. We were scheduled to leave for home first thing on Sunday morning, but my mom said that if the U.S. won, we would change our travel plans and go to the rally.

While all the celebrations were taking place after the game, I said "I guess we're staying for the rally." My mom agreed.

So on Sunday morning, instead of rushing off to catch our plane, we went down to the adidas Hospitality Suite for some breakfast. The reps from adidas were starting to take down the posters of their sponsored players and offered to give one each to Nicole and me.

The double-sided posters show Kristine Lilly on one side and Shannon MacMillan on the other. They include photos from when they were each little kids, along with recent action shots. They were so cute and really showed off the adidas theme from their "There From the Start!!" advertising campaign.

Later, we took a cab to the Los Angeles Convention Center for the rally. When we arrived, there were already several hundred people waiting near a small stage outside in the bright sun. We went inside in search of a water fountain and could see the players having their photos taken and being interviewed in a large room.

A crowd of people was trying to talk their way past the security guard, but she wouldn't let anyone in. I asked my parents if I could try to use my press pass for some more player comments. They both said yes.

I had to shove my way through the crowd, and when I got to the front, the security guard told me the room was for press only. I showed her my press pass, which really surprised her, "Oh! You are the press." She gave me a sticker that said "PRESS" on it and I went in.

The players were just sitting around, surrounded by reporters, talking. First, I went up to Joy Fawcett and another reporter was talking to her, so I just stuck my recorder in front of Joy and started to record her comments. I didn't have any questions for her, since I didn't expect another opportunity for comments.

Next, I went over to Carla Overbeck, listened to her and recorded some of her comments. I saw Danielle Fotopoulos and said "Hi!" to her. Like all the other players, she looked so happy and tired! I noticed they were all wearing their gold medals.

Then I went over to Julie Foudy, to tell her I thought she was "Foudious" during the game, but another reporter was already talking to her. As I approached them with tape recorder in hand, backpack over my shoulder and media pass hanging from my neck, the reporter asked Julie "Who's this?" I guess he never saw a junior reporter before.

Julie looked over at me and said "Oh that's Leah! She's the best of the bunch of ya'!" I was so excited that Julie recognized me from the day before. How cool!

But, before I had a chance to talk with her, Aaron Heifetz, the press officer, announced that it was time for the rally and that everyone had to leave the room. We were paraded outside where all the fans were waiting, into a special area with seats for the media right in front of the stage. I sat in the first row, which was great, because I had a perfect view of the whole rally.

After some opening comments, the team's co-captains, Julie Foudy and Carla Overbeck were introduced. Then Julie introduced the whole team, adding a funny comment about each player. For Brandi Chastain, she said "The one with the uncanny knack for taking her clothes off!" Lorrie Fair and Tiffany Roberts were called "The two Spice Girls."

For Mia Hamm, the crowd starting yelling, "Mia! Mia! Mia!" and Julie said, "Who is this one? I forgot her name. Who is this?" This time, the crowd screamed at her loudly "MIA!" Julie said, "Oh yeah. Mia Hamm." It was really funny, I took some pictures with my new digital camera, but unfortunately, I didn't think of turning on my tape recorder. Then they left to catch a plane for New York, with all the fans taking pictures and slapping high-fives with them.

World Cup Champions at the Victory Rally in Los Angeles.

Julie Foudy takes pictures of the press and the crowd with her fancy camera.

Our National Team was everywhere: newspaper headlines, television appearances, and within a week, all over the magazine covers, including *Sports Illustrated, Time, Newsweek*, and *People*. As a team, they went to the White House to meet President Clinton. Afterwards, they flew with First Lady Hillary Clinton onboard Air Force One to the Kennedy Space Center to see a shuttle launch.

And of course, they made a bunch of public appearances, with thousands of fans of all ages asking for autographs. Our National Team was an "overnight" sensation, but only after years of hard work and practice!

Then it was my turn to write my last story for the *St. Petersburg Times* as a junior reporter for the X-Team. But who knows? Maybe I'll be back in the future as a professional journalist.

Enter
GATE   SEC   ROW   SEAT
  F   17   5   104

Saturday, July 10,1999
Rose Bowl
10:30 a.m. Kickoff

USA
99   EVENT
         17

Third Place Game
Ceremony/Final Game

$110.00   Category I
Rose Bowl, Los Angeles

THIS IS MY GAME

F I F A
WOMEN'S
WORLD
CUP USA 99

WATCH ME PLAY

TERMS AND CONDITIONS

The kick of a lifetime

■ For one soccer fan and the U.S. Soccer team,
this was a real win-win occasion. Two contests proved victorious.

By LEAH LAUBER
Times X-Team

It's funny how things work out sometimes. A few months ago, I read an article in a soccer magazine announcing the "Color Is a Kick" photo contest sponsored by Hewlett-Packard, a big computer company. The challenge was for kids 12 to 15 to show in a single soccer photograph these qualities: speed, accuracy and no compromises.

The grand prize included a trip for four to Los Angeles for the Women's World Cup finals, a Hewlett-Packard digital camera and other cool computer equipment.

Earlier this year, I had the opportunity to attend the women's national soccer team residency camp in Orlando, and I had shot about two rolls of film of the team practicing. There was one frame I thought might have a good chance of winning.

Every day, I tore through the mail, hoping there would be a letter telling me I had won. Every night, I would check my e-mail, hoping for congratulations. Every time the phone rang, I would jump to answer it, hoping to hear those magic words. After a few weeks of waiting patiently, I was losing my patience.

Please see **SOCCER** 4D

Lauber family photo

X-Team member Leah Lauber is red, white and blue all over in her support for the U.S. women's soccer team. She still can't believe she got to attend the historymaking game between the United States and China last month in California.

Soccer from 3D

Finally, on a Friday night just two weeks before the finals, the phone rang. "Leah, it's for you!" my dad yelled.

He already knew I had won, so he had his camera out, loaded, with the flash turned on, ready to take my picture as I received the news.

The phone call was from Jules Andres of Hewlett-Packard, calling to congratulate me as a grand prize winner. I was so excited, I started screaming! "I'm going to L.A.!!!!" I was never so excited in my life.

Two weeks later, when we arrived in California at the beautiful Park Hyatt in Century City, Hewlett-Packard had the four winning photos enlarged into posters on display in the lobby.

On Friday, my dad and I went to the U.S. National Team practice at the Rose Bowl, even though I was the only one with a press pass. (They let him in as my chaperone!) On my way to the locker room for interviews, I saw Danielle Fotopoulos, who is from Tampa. I had interviewed her in December and again in May at the training camp. "Leah, what are YOU doing here?" she said.

I explained that I won the Hewlett-Packard photo contest and the grand prize was the trip to L.A. for the finals. I asked her to sign a copy of the winning photo, because she's in it. She congratulated me and I went to get the other players in the photo (Michelle Akers, Shannon MacMillan and Kate Sobrero) to autograph it as well.

Back at the hotel, we made posters for the game. My dad's said, "Real Men Love Women's Soccer!!" My sister Nicole's said, "Awesome Brandi Chastain," since ABC was broadcasting the game. I made a giant red heart and wrote "Tampa Bay Loves Danielle!"

On Saturday we went to the Rose Bowl, where my mom painted my face. Our tickets were great, about 15 rows behind the U.S. bench. George Fotopoulos, Danielle's husband, was sitting one row behind us and a few seats over. Before the game, I held up my "Tampa Bay Loves Danielle!" poster. George gave me a thumbs up and took my picture with the poster. So now, I might be in Danielle's photo album!

Finally came the moment I was dreaming about, the start of the Women's World Cup finals with 90,184 other people screaming their lungs out. Although it was hot, very hot,

very very hot, I loved every second and I still can't believe I was there, witnessing history. Both teams played tough throughout the entire first half. You could tell that the game was going to be a nail-biter and come right down to the final whistle.

The game was intense for all the fans in the stadium, so I can't even imagine what the team members felt like. We were nervous right down to Brandi's winning penalty kick. As soon as Brandi scored, we were jumping up and down and screaming. The United States had just won the Women's World Cup!

After the awards ceremony, I got to interview some of the players, Kristine Lilly, Briana Scurry, Julie Foudy, Cindy Parlow and Tiffeny Milbrett. I also took photos of the players with the digital camera Hewlett-Packard gave me. It's really cool, because once you take the picture, you can see it on the screen and either save it or record over it. I can download it to my computer, send it over e-mail to friends or print it out. Way cool!

At a rally at the Los Angeles Convention Center for the U.S. team on Sunday, I approached Julie Foudy, who was talking with another reporter, who asked Julie who I was. "Oh, that's Leah, she's the best of the bunch of ya." Wow, Julie Foudy knows my name!

If I hadn't decided to enter that photo contest, there wouldn't have been a chance to win it and have the greatest, coolest, most incredible once-in-a-lifetime experience of my short life!

Leah Lauber, 12, will be in the seventh grade at St. Jude Cathedral School in St. Petersburg.

Photo by LEAH LAUBER

Leah snapped this photo of members of the women's national soccer team at a camp in Orlando earlier this year. The photo won her a trip to the world championship.

- 13 -
Looking Back - What's it all mean?

As the months passed, my favorite team continued to become well-known stars and they received too many awards to count. There were individual awards, like Mia Hamm winning ESPN's "Female Athlete of the Year." There were major team awards, with them earning both *Sports Illustrated's* and ESPN's "Team of the Year." Winning the Women's World Cup was even recognized as the "Top Sports Story of the Year."

Photos of Brandi Chastain celebrating her winning penalty kick were published around the world and defined a moment in women's sports history. The success of the Women's World Cup even helped launch, in April, 2001, the Women's United Soccer Association (WUSA), a professional women's soccer league in the United States.

And for me, well, what twelve-year-old girl could even imagine having everything, and I do mean everything, fall into place to create a true once-in-a-lifetime chance to witness sports history?

It was an awful lot of hard work, but it was also an incredibly fun experience. I learned the value of commitment and persistence, not only by watching and enjoying the success of my heroes, but also by being able to experience a similar, yet much smaller type of success.

But with all the hard work, I was also very fortunate, maybe even lucky at times. I visited my friend, Jenelle, when she happened to be writing her application letter to the *St. Petersburg Times* X-Press Team. Then I was fortunate to be accepted.

Who could have predicted that Danielle Fotopoulos would come to my club for a clinic - we had never had anyone like that in my six years playing there - and that I'd be able to interview her for my first story?

It was pure luck that the National Team game, originally scheduled for Gainesville, was switched to Tampa at the last minute, allowing me to attend, interview eight players and write my story "Soccer Diaries" for the *St. Petersburg Times.*

Looking back, I was lucky even when it rained and we arrived late for my first trip to the training center. If I had seen practice that day and written my story on what it takes to be a world-class athlete, I probably wouldn't have planned another trip a few weeks later.

Then I was fortunate to see the announcement for the Hewlett-Packard kid's photo contest, BEFORE we drove over to that second practice, so I knew to take pictures that day. Lucky for me, Mia went on a scoring drought, followed by a scoring streak and I wound up on the field, twenty feet from her, when she broke the scoring record.

Then, winning the Hewlett-Packard photo contest, going to Los Angeles, and being able to use my media credentials to get interviews was the best experience any girl of any age could ever hope to have.

And it all started with a love of reading, which led to a love of writing, combined with a love of soccer, which led to a love of the players on the U.S. National Team.

Isn't it funny how things work out sometimes?

Section 3

Unedited Interviews, Quotes and Comments from the U.S. Women's National Team

February 27, 1999
Friendly Match vs. Finland
University of Tampa, Florida

I knew I wouldn't be providing game coverage, and since I wanted to interview as many players as possible, I asked the same three questions of each player, recording their answers for future articles.

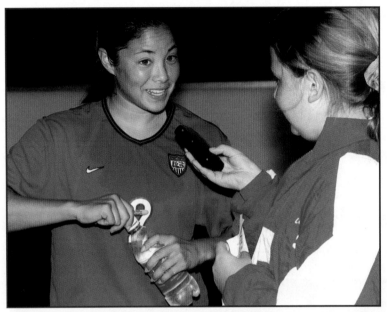

Lorrie Fair, Defender

Leah: Since the Women's World Cup is in the United States, what effect do you think it will have on the growth of soccer?

Lorrie: The effect it will have? Well, the thing about that, is the Olympics was a huge event and I think a lot people could see what we can do in terms of women's soccer. The Olympics was a whole bunch of events, but the Women's World Cup is just women's soccer. I think with the fan support we have in the United States, I think it's the best thing in the world. And for us to host the biggest women's event in history, is a tribute to our fans and our country. Just the fact that we can do it. I think it will spark a lot of young people to play soccer.

Leah: Why is the Women's World Cup such a big deal?

Lorrie: The Women's World Cup? It's the world championship! If you can imagine being the best team in the world, that's why it's such a big deal. And the fact that it's being publicized so much, a lot of people didn't know about the '91 Cup and a lot of people didn't know about the '95 Cup. This one, we're trying to get everyone to know about it, so we can get everyone in to the games.

Leah: Do you think the Women's World Cup is something we should all care about?

Lorrie: Absolutely! This is the biggest women's event in history of any sport, so it's something we should definitely, especially as women, care about.

Joy Fawcett, Defender

Leah: Since the Women's World Cup is in the United States, what effect do you think it will have on the growth of soccer?

Joy: I think it will have a huge effect on the growth of soccer. It's the biggest event for soccer in the world and the stadiums are going to be full. I think, once they see how popular the game is and with all the games on TV, everyone will be able to watch it and be exposed to it. I think it will definitely grow.

Leah: Why is the Women's World Cup such a big deal?

Joy: Soccer is the most popular sport in the world and it is a soccer event - the championship of soccer.

Leah: Do you think the Women's World Cup is something we should all care about?

Joy: Definitely! Everyone should care about the Women's World Cup and women's soccer. We're a fun team to watch. We're a fun team to be around and soccer is a great sport, so I think everyone should care about it. It's good for kids, and more kids play soccer than any other sport.

Briana Scurry, Goalkeeper

Leah: Since the Women's World Cup is in the United States, what effect do you think it will have on the growth of soccer?

Briana: It will have a big effect on the growth of soccer. Just like in the Olympics in '96 when we won and when soccer really got big and lots of little girls started playing. I think it will have the same effect, having the United States host the Women's World Cup. I think it will be even bigger than it is now.

Leah: Why is the Women's World Cup such a big deal?

Briana: It's a big deal because they are trying to stage it in major events in major cities. They are trying to make football stadiums filled to get people to watch women's athletics. I think it's going be really important.

Leah: Do you think the Women's World Cup is something we should all care about?

Briana: Oh absolutely! It's definitely something we should care about. Are you kidding me? All women should care about it. And men should care about it because women care about it. It's going to be huge and a breakthrough event. I think it's very important for society to come out and support us.

Cindy Parlow, Forward

Leah: Since the Women's World Cup is in the United States, what effect do you think it will have on the growth of soccer?

Cindy: I think soccer is just going to get bigger. I think the Olympics was one thing and we had 76,000 people at the final game. I think that is just a precursor of what the Women's World Cup is going to be like. I think we are going to sell out the stadiums and I think it's going to be the biggest event in '99.

Leah: Why is the Women's World Cup such a big deal?

Cindy: It is the only huge championship where soccer is on the stage - it's the only sport on the stage. You had the Olympics and that's a huge event, but that's every sport. The Women's World Cup is just women's soccer and that's it. It's the most popular sport in the world and we need to make it the most popular sport in the United States also.

Leah: Do you think the Women's World Cup is something we should all care about?

Cindy: Oh definitely! I think that everyone that is here today and watched it on TV knows how exciting this game can be. It's just a great game to watch and a great game to play. Once people come out and see one game, they are hooked for life.

Shannon MacMillan, Midfielder

Leah: Since the Women's World Cup is in the United States, what effect do you think it will have on the growth of soccer?

Shannon: I think it will have a big effect, because basically, everyone will be able to see women's soccer and see what it is all about and the growth that it's been developing, how we've progressed through the years. Hopefully, people will see that women's soccer is not too far off from men's soccer.

Leah: Why is the Women's World Cup such a big deal?

Shannon: It's a big deal because it's the biggest tournament held for women's soccer and it's big enough for us and for the growth of soccer. If we succeed in this tournament, it will only be better for us and hopefully, we will start a professional league off of it.

Leah: Do you think the Women's World Cup is something we should all care about?

Shannon: Oh definitely! I think anyone that is younger and growing up and involved in soccer, this is only going to be a starting point for them. As they get older, they can look into the future and think professional.

Christie Pearce
Defender

As you can see from the photo, I DID interview Christie, but somehow, I must have pushed the pause button on my tape recorder by mistake. I have none of her quotes, which was very disappointing, because this was the only time I interviewed her.

So, Christie, if you ever read this, thank you for kindly answering my questions and I'm sorry for my rookie mistake.

Mia Hamm, Forward

Leah: Since the Women's World Cup is in the United States, what effect do you think it will have on the growth of soccer?
Mia: I think it's going to give us a lot more exposure and hopefully, young girls will get excited about it, and maybe this will lead to a professional league.

Leah: Why is the Women's World Cup such a big deal?
Mia: For soccer, it's our greatest sporting event and I think what we are trying to do with it here in the United States, is try to make it a breakthrough event for women. Make it the largest sporting event ever, in history for women, not just for soccer, but for women's sports in general.

Leah: Do you think the Women's World Cup is something we should all care about?
Mia: Definitely! I think anyone who wants their daughters or themselves, their sisters, their aunts, their grandmothers to have more opportunities, I think this is an important event to get out there and support the sport and support the women that participate.

Julie Foudy, Midfielder

Leah: Since the Women's World Cup is in the United States, what effect do you think it will have on the growth of soccer?
Julie: It's going to be great because all 32 games will be on television. It's going to be in big stadiums and there is going to be a lot of enthusiasm. So you're going to attract a larger crowd of people watching soccer, not just your hard core soccer fans that come now. So what you're going to see, is a lot of kids watching it, a lot of girls watching it. And hopefully, you're going to see an increase in the amount of girls playing soccer and wanting to play soccer.

Leah: Why is the Women's World Cup such a big deal?
Julie: It only happens every four years and for soccer players, that's like the pinnacle of your career, the peak of your career, just like you would have a world championship for skiing, or for figure skating or what else. For soccer, this is it and it happens every four years just like the men's, it's the highest you can reach as a soccer player.

Leah: Do you think the Women's World Cup is something we should all care about?
Julie: Oh, yes, definitely care about. You know why? It's going to open a lot of doors for young girls out there. They're going to see not just sports, they're going to see the opportunity of women doing things they love and making a living out of it.

April 17, 1999
Training Center, Sanford, Florida

As we drove to the training center, I was able to prepare more in-depth questions. The focus was on practice and what it takes to be a world class athlete. But with nasty weather and traffic delays, we arrived late. I was only able to interview four players and the team's press officer. But my tape recorder didn't work for Lorrie Fair - oops!

Tiffeny Milbrett, Forward

Leah: How often do you practice individually or with the team?
Tiffeny: Do you want me to include my name first? Okay. My name is Tiffeny Milbrett. You spell that T-I-F-F-E-N-Y . . .M-I-L-B-R-E-T-T. Well, since we are down here in residency, we train pretty much every day and then, depending on how tired we are, we have either the fifth or sixth or seventh day off. So we train for five days or six days, then have a day off.

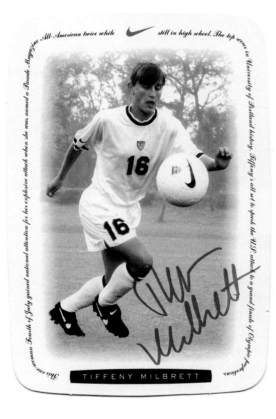

TIFFENY MILBRETT

Leah: Who do you think the toughest competition will be in the Women's World Cup?
Tiffeny: I think whenever you have a World Cup, every team is going to be tough. I think we are going to have a tough bracket, we are going to have a tough time getting out of our bracket. We want to come out on top, number one, so that's going to be tough. Then I think any team we encounter in the Quarterfinals or the Semis, and hopefully the Finals, is going to be tough. I think when it's a World Cup, it's the kind of competition where anything goes, like all teams are ready to beat you. So I think all the teams are going to be dangerous.

Leah: Is your practice hard?
Tiffeny: Practice is very hard. I think the one thing that is hard about it, it's exhausting. Because we train very hard. We train at 100 percent of what we have, everyday. When we do that every day, it's really exhausting.

Leah: Is it hard to stay focused?
Tiffeny: I think when we are down here, as a group, as a team, no, it's not hard to stay focused. It's when we start going on the road, when we start to get tired, that's when it's hard to stay focused. In general, when we are down here, we are here to prepare for the World Cup. It's not hard to stay focused.

Leah: What do you do at practice?
Tiffeny: They vary. Any day can be completely different. One day we could do just ball skills or you could just completely work on small-sided games the next practice, or we can do shooting one practice. We work on everything. Especially when we have six months before the World Cup to prepare everyday, that's a lot of practices and we have to work on a lot of things.

Leah: What do you do when you're not practicing?
Tiffeny: When we're not practicing, like I said before, because we train so hard, it depends on our energy level when we're done with practice. Some people go shopping, go to the mall, movies, get food, go to a sandwich shop, go to Starbucks or anything like that. It really depends on our legs and our energy level.

Leah: If you weren't on the National Team, what would you be doing?
Tiffeny: I have no idea. I really don't. I've always been a soccer player and I've always been an athlete, so I think I would be doing something athletic.

Brandí Chastain, Defender

Leah: How often do you practice individually or with the team?

Brandi: I guess you could look at that two ways. At this point of the year, in preparation of the Women's World Cup, we practice every day, up to two hours on the field and another hour or so in the weight room. It can be up to three hours a day, depending on the kind of training we're doing for the day. We usually have every seventh day off, so sometimes seven out of seven days a week, and sometimes six.

Leah: Who do you think the toughest competition will be this World Cup?

Brandi: Well, this World Cup, I think if you look at all the teams that are involved, it could be any, any one of the handful of teams that will be playing for the championship. Norway is always tough. China is always tough. Brazil has improved over the last four years. Germany is always in the championship game for the European championship. So there are four or five teams that I think could be the champions of this tournament. I think we have a lot of work ahead of us.

Leah: Is the practice hard?

Brandi: We always have a point of saying when the training gets really hard, that no other team in the world trains as hard as we do, 'cause we have the best players. I definitely feel that after a hard day of competition here, we've definitely trained harder than any game we'll ever have in the World Cup, so our training is pretty tough.

Leah: What do you guys do at the practices?

Brandi: That's a pretty tough question, because it depends on what we are focusing on for the day. We have a lot of areas that we are focusing on lately. Right now, we are focusing on shooting and finishing, and goal scoring opportunities, so we've been in front of the goal. Before that, we were changing our line-up, so we were working on tactical things like positioning, where players need to be defensively, heading on-goal, heading for clearances in front of the goal. Now that we are closer to the World Cup, we are focusing more on the goal and scoring goals.

Leah: What do you do when you're not practicing?

Brandi: Well, sometimes. . . well, a lot of the times, when we are down here in Florida, we like to go golfing, so we spend a lot of time on the golf course, and we all enjoy being together. As much as we spend time on the field, we like to spend time together, so we'll go to the movies, go shopping a lot. We do things that every normal teenage girl would do.

Leah: If you weren't on the National Team, what do you think you would be doing?

Brandi: Well, there was a time between '91, when I first joined the National Team, and '96, when I wasn't on the National Team, when I became an assistant coach at the university level. I would most likely be a coach in college.

Mía Hamm, Forward

Leah: How often do you practice individually or with the team?
Mia: Well, right now, we go about six days a week, anywhere from two to six hours a day.

Leah: Who do you think the toughest competition will be?
Mia: Probably China, Norway, Germany and Brazil, but everybody in the tournament is going to be tough.

Leah: Is the practice hard?
Mia: Yeah, some days are harder than others, but they're all pretty intense and fun.

Leah: What do you guys do at the practices?
Mia: We do different things, we do technical skills, you know, trapping, dribbling, passing. We worked on a lot of tactical organization, working on our defensive shape, making sure that up front, in the mid-field, and in the back, we're all working together.

Leah: What do you do when you're not practicing?
Mia: I go shopping. I babysit Carla's little son, 'cause he's fun, but I play golf, read.

Leah: If you weren't on the National Team, what do you think you would be doing?
Mia: I don't know. I've never had that opportunity to NOT be on this team.

Aaron Heifetz, Press Officer

Leah: What is your official title?
Aaron: Press Officer for the Women's National Team

Leah: How many tickets have you sold already?
Aaron: We have sold 325,000 tickets, an average of about 20,000 per event. Every game is in double-headers, so for each of the double-headers, about 20,000 tickets.

Leah: Is that how many you expected?
Aaron: No. It's more than we expected at this point. We only expected to sell, well, let's put it this way, projections at the beginning of the ticket sales were for 386,000, so we sold almost that right now, with two months to go.

Leah: How many press credentials do you expect to issue and from how many countries?
Aaron: Another good question. The deadline was April 9th, and we received over 1,500 credential applications, and we expect to receive even more, so when the tournament starts, about 2,000 from 26 countries all around the world.

Leah: How many countries will the games be televised in?
Aaron: Have you been reading my press releases? Right now, it's 66 countries around the world, for the potential audience of one billion people. It could be more by the time the tournament starts. Some countries haven't purchased TV rights yet, but it should be over 70 by the time the tournament kicks off.

Leah: How long has the women's team been practicing together for the Women's World Cup?
Aaron: The core of the team has been together for ten to thirteen years, and you can kind of say that the whole time has been preparing for a World Cup in your home country. But for this particular World Cup, and for this particular residency camp, they've been here in Florida since January 3rd of '99. With week-long breaks in there every month, and of course, we travel on the road for games as well.

May 21, 1999
Last Day of Residency Camp
Sanford, Florida

Since I was still working on my "world-class athlete" story, some of my questions related to practice. Other questions related to the Olympics or where the players enjoyed playing.

Brandi Chastain, Defender

Leah: Do you practice when you aren't in residency camp?
Brandi: Yes. I probably play or practice soccer every day with my friends or by myself. If I can't practice every day, then every other day.

Leah: Do you practice on your day off?
Brandi: If we have an extended break, like more than one day, I will practice. If it's one day, maybe I'll go for a light jog and keep it at that.

Leah: You're on a team that's the best in the world, so why do you practice so hard?
Brandi: Because we know that every team out there in the World Cup this summer is going to be gunning and playing their best when they face us, so we have to be as good as we can be.

Leah: What is the best country you played in?
Brandi: Ooh that's a tough one. In terms of best soccer fans or in terms of the nicest place?

Leah: Nicest place?
Brandi: Nicest place. I liked Portugal a lot but I also like playing soccer in Germany because their tradition for soccer is pretty strong, so that was a fun place.

Leah: What is the worst country you ever played in?
Brandi: Ooh. No comment. They're have been some bad ones, but each country has it's good qualities, so there aren't any bad countries.

Leah: What is your favorite thing about being on the national team?
Brandi: That I get to play the game that I love, everyday, with my best friends.

Leah: In 1996, when the Olympic gold medal was placed around your neck, what was that like?
Brandi: It was like a dream come true and I couldn't believe how heavy it was. I was amazed by the weight of the gold medal.

Leah: You've been in residency camp for five months, do you think that you, personally, are ready?
Brandi: I think I will be ready come June 19th, we still have a little less than a month, so . . . hopefully, I'll be at my peak performance on the 19th.

Leah: What about the team?
Brandi: The team's definitely going in the right direction. We're not quite at our peak, but we will be come June 19th.

Bríana Scurry, Goalkeeper

Leah: How do you practice when you aren't in residency camp?
Briana: I basically just do lifting when I'm not here in residency camp. I'm assuming you mean when there's no residency at all, not when we're on our breaks. I just do lifting and sometimes I go off for some crosses, I don't play a whole lot of soccer and I don't have a team to play on when I'm at home.

Leah: Do you practice on your day off?
Briana: Rarely. I mean my day off is my day off. You know what I'm saying? My practice time is my practice time and my day off is my day off. I have to keep them separate, otherwise I'll go crazy.

Leah: You're on a team that's the best in the world, so why do you practice so hard?
Briana: 'Cause you got to work hard to stay the best. Other teams are working hard to catch up with you and if you're the best and you don't practice hard, you're going to lose ground. So you have to practice a lot, even though you're the best.

Leah: What is the best country you played in?
Briana: Best I've played in. I would have said Australia but we ended up in a kinda backwood area where nothing was happening. France was pretty cool. I'd have to say France.

Leah: What is the worst country you've ever played in?
Briana: Germany. It rained. Probably ten of the twelve days we were there. That was horrible.

Leah: What is your favorite thing about being on the national team?
Briana: Just the relationships, the friendships. It's a big family here and it's exciting and it helps when we win too. That probably is a big boost. But just getting to know people and feel that I can count on them for anything, is what I think is the biggest asset.

Leah: What makes the U.S. team so strong?
Briana: I think what makes us so strong is that we are all very good individual athletes, but we all work so hard for each other, that makes us better. I don't want to let anybody down. Nobody wants to let me down. I think it goes all over the team, so I think the whole accountability asset is what makes us strong.

Leah: In 1996, when the Olympic gold medal was placed around your neck, what was that like?
Briana: That was unbelievable, that was a dream come true for me. I had been dreaming about being in the Olympics for, up until that point, about 17 years or so, since I was really young. It was an incredible feeling for me, because my family was there and my friends were there. We won it at home, so it was the most unbelievable experience.

Leah: You've been in residency camp for five months, do you think you personally are ready for the Women's World Cup?
Briana: I think I'm ready. I think I've been ready for about a month now. I'm ready for camp to be over with and let's get on with the World Cup already.

Leah: What about the team?
Briana: We're coming along. We're doing really well right now. I think we are ready too, as a team, but the next month or so will be good for us and by the World Cup, we'll be running on all cylinders.

Danielle Fotopoulos, Forward

Leah: Do you practice when you aren't in residency camp?
Danielle: Yeah, I practice year round, always with club teams, doing what I can to improve myself.

Leah: Do you practice on your day off?
Danielle: Yes, I do. Not all of them, but most of them. After we are training, I probably take a day or two, maybe, but yeah, I train on my days off.

Leah: You're on a team that's the best in the world, so why do you practice so hard?
Danielle: 'Cause in order to achieve your goals, and get where you want to be, you have to continue to practice and when you're playing on a team so good, you have to keep your performance up.

Leah: What is the best country you played in?
Danielle: The United States. . . The United States is the best country, because obviously we're from here, so we get good crowds.

Leah: The worst?
Danielle: I don't know. Anywhere we go, we're welcome. I don't think any one country is worse than the other.

Leah: What is your favorite thing about being on the national team?
Danielle: I guess just playing at this level. I love playing with the girls and the team. The team is really great.

Leah: What makes the U.S. team so strong?
Danielle: I think the fact that everybody trains so hard together. On our off days, people are training and working, just playing hard together. I think too, the unity of the family, we're kind of a family.

Leah: What does it feel like to be in a major event like the Women's World Cup?
Danielle: Great. It's something that I've been working for all my life, so it's a good feeling.

Leah: You've been in residency camp for five months, do you think that you personally are ready?
Danielle: Yes, I do. I feel that if I am called to perform on the field, I will be ready to go.

Leah: What about the team?
Danielle: Yeah. We're ready. We've been training together for five months, we've sacrificed a lot for this event, and we're ready to go.

Leah: How do you feel knowing you made the team?
Danielle: AWESOME! I'm very excited about it. I'm excited to be playing for my country.

After Mia Hamm broke the international scoring record with her 108th goal, my dad said I wouldn't be able to interview her one-on-one. He suggested I position myself right next to Mia and to keep my tape recorder rolling as she answered the questions from a pack of reporters. The questions really jumped from one topic to another as the reporters bombarded Mia.

Mia Hamm, Super - Scorer

Q. How do you feel about breaking the scoring record?
Mia: It feels pretty good! This was a special moment and Orlando has been our home for the past, well, the last three times we were down here. And the fans were awesome tonight, and they just support us the whole way, kind of emotional at times, but they really helped us through some tough times, and I'm really glad I could do it here.

Q. What does the win over Brazil mean to the team?
Mia: Well, it means a lot to us in terms of our confidence. We feel that if we want to get to the final, we're going to have to face Brazil. As you saw tonight, they have some tremendous personalities, that can just shred apart defenses in teams. I think a 3-0 result - we'll take any day against Brazil.

Q. The third goal was scored after Brazil cleared the ball deep into the stands and the ball was put into play before the Brazilian defense was ready. Your comment, please.
Mia: It was good for us, because I think what happened is, towards the end it became so emotional and we kind of kept our cool and stayed focused. That last goal, it was an unbelievable goal by Brandi, with Kristine putting it across the stage. You know they weren't organized, and us being level-headed, putting the ball into the play quickly, and getting a cross was a factor from us being so level-headed.

Q. Is your team ready for the Women's World Cup?
Mia: Right now, I think our team just wants to play the best that we can, just take every game one at a time. When we play Denmark, they have to be our focus. We can't think about Nigeria, we can't think about North Korea, we have to focus on Denmark. Right now, we are just trying to work things out, obviously from this game, we still need to work some. But we are building every day and I'm just excited about the potential for this team.

Q. What does the record mean to you now, and what do you think it will mean in the future?
Mia: I don't know . . . It means a lot to me right now, but it will probably mean a lot more to me once I stop playing and kind of look back on my career. Right now, I just love the fact that I could be here and share it with my teammates. They are a big part of all these goals, and the fact that they all ran out on the field was awesome. I don't know what everybody was saying. Everybody was screaming at once, but they were just telling me how awesome it was and how proud they were of me.

Q. Before the goal, you had a wide-open opportunity to score, but missed. Did you think you'd get another chance like that?

Mia: I can't be thinking about that during the game. I had a chance. I should have put it away, I didn't. I had to get over it and get back into the game, because Brazil, being the team that they are, they serve one ball long, and they are coming at our defense. If I don't get in good defensive shape, than I can really hurt my team.

Q. Any special feelings about breaking the record here in Orlando?

Mia: It's special, because the people in Orlando, where we are living, Lake Mary Heathrow, have done so much for us, especially this time around. They really opened their arms and have done so many wonderful things for us. I know most of the people who helped us are here tonight, that's kind of our way of saying "Thank You" for all the great times we've had here.

Q. Does breaking the scoring record help your confidence?

Mia: Well, it definitely helps the confidence, because when you are a forward, you wanna score goals and create opportunities. When you aren't doing that consistently, you kind of get down on yourself. You don't really listen to what everyone else is saying, but it does get you sometimes. But the team is so supportive, and some comments were like, "We didn't even know Mia hadn't scored in that long." That says a lot, to what they think of me as a player, they think I'm still contributing. Confidence is one of those things you build every day. Right now, I think I'm going in a positive way. I have to keep building.

Q. Can you describe the goal?

Mia: I didn't touch it very well. I thought I was leaning back, but I guess it just went right through her legs. It was almost like the first time, when I hit her in the legs, so I was lucky that this one got through. A great ball coming in from Cindy. It's funny, we had something similar when she passed to Brandi inside and it was called offsides. I was on the outside again and this time she touched it outside, cause I was running forward. What a great build up and that ball came across and Cindy's one touch back. That was awesome!

Q. Is the team ready for the World Cup?
Mia: We're getting there. You know, we still have a good three-and-a-half weeks and there are some things we need to fine-tune. I think people are getting excited and the team is getting a lot closer. We're getting fitter, and we're building confidence, so we're excited for the tournament. We know it's going to be tough.

Q. Who do you think will make it to the Finals?
Mia: Pick a team. They will be in the Finals. There are so many great teams out there. Brazil, Norway, China, Germany. That's what's great about this tournament, any team on any given day can be in the Finals.

Q. Your father and your husband are here tonight. Do they see many games?
Mia: Well, my dad sees a lot of the games on TV, he doesn't get to come in person. I was glad he was here tonight. Probably the same with my husband. He also sees a lot of games on TV.

Q. How many games have they seen you play?
Mia: I don't know. Maybe 40 games.

Q. What does it mean that they were here tonight?
Mia: Both of them have been so supportive, my dad since day one. He loves this game and he loves this team and it means a lot that he could be here. Christian, I'm gone all the time, and I've never heard him complain about it.

After the team went into the locker room, we were getting ready to leave, when I saw Coach Tony DiCicco sitting on some stadium steps, eating pizza. When he finished his late dinner, I asked him if I could interview him. He agreed, so I pulled out my notebook and tape recorder.

Coach DiCicco congratulates Mia after her 108th goal.

Tony DiCicco, Coach

Leah: How hard do you work the team?
Coach DiCicco: Well, we try to work hard on some days and easy on others, so it's not hard work every day. It's high-leveled concentration every day - but it's not physically hard every day, cause that would just wear everyone out and it wouldn't be fun to play. It has to be fun to play.

Leah: What kind of things do you make them practice?
Coach DiCicco: We practice individual skills, but we also practice team coordination, team tactics and then we also practice set plays, like dead ball situations, corner kicks and free kicks, etc.

Leah: What do you look for when picking people for the team?
Coach DiCicco: I look for players with character, players that I can trust that, even when they aren't with the team, they will practice by themselves. I also look for players that have a special quality. Maybe they're fast, maybe they're leaders, maybe they're great headers, but they have to have a special quality. When you get all those special qualities together, you can piece them together. It's kind of like when you put a puzzle together.

July 9, 1999
Rose Bowl Locker Room
Pasadena, California

The day before the Women's World Cup Finals, I felt like the luckiest girl in the world as I entered the locker room for interviews and quotes. Like the night when Mia Hamm broke the scoring record, I knew there would be a mob of reporters with great questions. My plan was to record the players' comments, but I also had a few questions of my own for individual players.

Kristine Lilly, Midfielder

Q. Besides a win, what do you want out of tomorrow's game?
Kristine: We haven't been thinking about it. But, I guess what we want is some more respect. Basically, we have done a lot for the game, to show what happens with this World Cup, how we played and the success. We want what's fair. That's all we ever asked for and that's all we ever wanted.

Leah: Were you ever overwhelmed by the number of people at a game?
Kristine: The first game of the World Cup was an overwhelming feeling for all of us, but once it was underway, we relaxed.

Leah: Are you nervous about the game tomorrow?
Kristine: No, I'm not nervous yet, but I always get nervous before any game, a natural nervousness which is healthy for all of us.

Leah: How do you like the adidas commercial of you?
Kristine: It's great! I think their whole concept - 'There From the Start' - is a great theme they have going. Besides, they picked a cute kid to represent me, so I liked it.

Leah: Did you wear adidas when you were younger?
Kristine: Yes! I've been wearing adidas since I was very little playing.

Sara Whalen, Midfielder

Q. Are you nervous that you must put on a great show to satisfy all your new fans?
Sara: No, we're not so much nervous and we're ready, I think, to put on our best show out there. I don't think we've done that yet. We're just excited.

Q. Are there any superstitions brought along the way that you, personally, or the team, will do tonight or in the morning before the game?
Sara: Not necessarily. There are things I've developed throughout the World Cup that always help a lot - like watching our imagery tapes. There are also certain songs I listen to that remind me of how hard I've worked through residency camp and the struggles we've put up with in the last five or six months. Those are the kind of feelings I want to go into those environments with, and I want to feel that I deserve to be where I am and we all deserve to be in the final game. We all know what we've done for it and we're all there to win it.

Q. What are the songs?
Sara: One that my roommate, Kate Sobrero, and I listened to through residency is "You Get What You Give" from The Radicals. That's a big one. It carried us through some hard times. We'd listen to it and it was one of our happy songs. It would get us in a good mood and get us excited to go out there and play again. We have a bunch of different fast songs to get us happy, because what we want to do, is have fun. That's what this team is all about.

Q. Tonight, will you get together as a team, go for a quick meeting, or go your separate ways?
Sara: One thing that's good about this team is that we hang out all the time together. We don't do it because we have to; we do it because we want to. Tonight, because everyone is a little tired and we have a big game tomorrow, we'll probably just get a movie in the hotel, or just play Scrabble because it's everyone's new favorite game right now. It's hard to tell, but I can tell you we'll probably all be together doing something.

Q. And what time has Tony posted to get up and down for breakfast for you?
Sara: Good question. Probably between 8:00 and 9:00 a.m. Some of the girls get up really early, but others, like myself, sleep as late as possible. So we can get down there whenever we want to. He's really good about making things flexible like that.

Q. Have you been to the West Coast before this trip?
Sara: A couple of times. We had that one game back in the Rose Bowl a couple of months ago but we didn't get to spend much time here. This past week, being here, was a lot of fun. I like the area. Weather's been great, except for yesterday.

Q: Are your parents here?
Sara: They flew in today. I'll just tell them to stop to visit, but the team doesn't like to have a lot of visitors. We want to try to keep focused for right now. They will probably stop by after dinner. That's pretty much it. They know what I'm focusing on. They don't take it personally.

Q. What does "LIA" mean?

Sara: That means Long Island Attitude. It's actually from my college days, when I came into UCONN as a freshman. I was really quiet but once you get to know me, I'm not a quiet person. I do have a little "bite" to myself. So one of the seniors nicknamed me "LIA" and, unfortunately I told Kate, and naturally she told everyone else. But I don't care. It's funny to me.

Leah: Are you nervous about the game tomorrow?

Sara: It's a nervous excitement. We trained so hard for this and we know we are going to play our best and we want to be successful. We're just excited to get on the field and have a good time.

Leah: Were you ever overwhelmed by the number of people at a game?

Sara: Yeah. I never played before as large a crowd as was at Giants Stadium - the opener. I was shocked to see all the people there. I knew what kind of numbers would be there, but I didn't know what it would look like or feel like. That was definitely huge for me. It was exciting, but once you start playing, it was just like any other game. You forget about the crowd. It was good.

Kate Sobrero, Defender

Q. Is there more pressure to win now that you've made it to the Finals?

Kate: The pressure's gone. Our whole goal was to get to the Finals. This tournament would not have been successful unless we did get to the Finals, so all the pressure is now gone.

Q. Pressure in what way? For you personally, or for the whole team?

Kate: No, as a whole. For the American public to embrace the sport and to get all the attention of what we're trying to do, is great. If we had lost early on, it wouldn't have happened. We knew what we had to do. Now that pressure is gone. We've gotten to the Finals and we're playing a team that's just as good as we are. So all the pressure is gone. It's time to play. We can forget all that "stuff."

Q. What do you expect from the Chinese?

Kate: They're organized. They're very quick. They always have a lot of numbers forward. They're very calculating. They move in swarms and they always have numbers around the ball. They are a very, very, very good team.

Q. Are they as athletic as Nigeria?

Kate: No team will ever be as athletic as Nigeria. Oh, my God, those women are all huge, fast women. They are quicker in some positions than we are.

Leah: Were you ever overwhelmed by the number of people at a game?

Kate: I've kind of 'tuned out,' because it is so overwhelming. I don't focus on it. It's too big to focus on.

Leah: Are you nervous about the game tomorrow?

Kate: No. I'm excited. I'll be a little bit nervous. Who wouldn't be? But, more than anything, I'm excited to play in it.

Leah: Is it true that you have to shave your head if Carla scores a goal?

Kate: That was a joke that got out of hand. Carla and I were joking about it and I was stupid and it got in the paper. I would never shave my head. I couldn't pull it off. It was just a big joke.

Leah: Last year, you weren't even on the National team and now you're a starting defender in the Women's World Cup. How does that feel?

Kate: It's pretty huge. I can't believe in a year, how much has happened. It's pretty exciting. I'm just glad I'm a part of it. In the beginning, I was just looking to make the team and I'm surprised I'm starting, but I'm happy for it.

Joy Fawcett, Defender

Q. How will you defend Sun Wen?
Joy: She's a very good playmaker and good at distributing the ball. We'll have to shut her down quickly, so she can't bring her other players into the game.

Q. Is she someone you should put someone 'on' to stick with her?
Joy: I don't know. That's the Coach's decision but he is considering it. We'll see. Maybe in the middle of the game he'll yell that out from the sidelines. That's his decision if she's having too much of an impact.

Q. Do you believe that's the way it will work?
Joy: I don't know. In the past games this year, we've been able to absorb her, so I don't think we need to, unless something happens.

Q. She seems to be peaking as the tournament goes on, some of her opponents say she's "unstoppable." Do you think she's at a place now that she hasn't been before?
Joy: Probably. I think most players are peaking at this time and I'm sure she's at her best, so we'll definitely have to focus on making sure that she's taken care of, whether it's one person or absorbing it throughout our team defense, making sure we cover for each other when we're on her.

Q. About the Chinese defense: their defensive attack is impressive, the way their defenders keep people apart, aiming forward. Can you talk about the way their team defenders come forward and the problems that causes?
Joy: In one of our earlier games, it caused a lot of problems where their defense and their midfielders were coming down one flank, leaving our outside defenders to be the ones attacking on the flank. We've addressed this situation and we're trying to make sure that their defenders can't get out of the attack as frequently as they'd like to.

Q. In terms of technical ability, for example, in holding the ball, China is the best in the world. But their finishing hasn't been that strong. Have they found that somewhere along the way?
Joy: It looks that way because they're putting their goals in. Five goals are a lot of goals in one game against Norway. So they've obviously worked on it and improved on it. We'll have to shut them down early and not allow them to shoot.

Leah: Have you ever been overwhelmed by the number of people at a game?
Joy: Probably when we first had those crowds in the Olympics, but a lot of us are used to it. We've played in front of big crowds before. It certainly gets you pumped up and inspires you to play harder.

Leah: Are you nervous about the game tomorrow?
Joy: Sometimes I get nervous when I think about it, but I won't get real nervous until right before the game.

Leah: In the Quarterfinals against Germany, was that the most important goal you ever scored?
Joy: Yes, I think so. It was a goal we needed to take us to the next game. It was win or lose so it was the winning goal. It was definitely one of the biggest goals I've scored.

Mía Hamm, Forward

Q. Can the U.S. team contain Sun Wen?
Mia: We can't let her pace us. When she's good, she's really good about her runs off the ball. She plays the ball. She's been playing so well for them lately. By "lately" - I mean the last three or four years. She's a threat and we need to contain her and definitely show her the respect she deserves.

Q. Do you think this will be the last World Cup appearance for a group of you or is the jury still out on that?
Mia: I don't think anyone has made any career decisions yet. We can't think about that now. All we've talked about is what people possibly will be doing after the World Cup, such as vacations. But we haven't talked about career decisions.

Q. One more for Mia. What do you think the team needs to improve before next year's Olympics?
Mia: We have to play tomorrow and that's where our focus is. The Olympics are so far away.

Q. What do you think the team has to work on in general? How can the team get better?
Mia: We can answer that question after tomorrow.

Shannon MacMillan, Midfielder

Q. You've been in residency since January. Is there a sense that it's almost over?

Shannon: It's been crazy. This was our last practice. "Wait a minute - it can't be here yet." Tony said before practice, "This is our goal to be here, July 10th." and we said "yeah, yeah." But now that we're here, it's all gone so fast, and here we are!

Q. What's your role tomorrow? Are there any changes?

Shannon: Good question. Tony hasn't given us a clue yet. We usually find out right after breakfast when he posts the starting line-up. I'm just ready for anything. Hopefully, I'll get a chance to start. I would just love to. I'd take that chance and run with it. I'll be out there going crazy. But if it means coming off the bench, I'm ready for that as well. It's going to take all 20 of us to wear these Chinese down. It's going to come down to which unit wants it more.

Q. You have big game experience, especially Olympic experience. How does that play a role tomorrow, possibly experience that Kate doesn't have?

Shannon: It's huge. Just going into the Germany game when we were tied, Tony and Lauren were like "go do it again." It was once-in-a-lifetime. I don't know what I can do out there and to step in and get the cross into Joy, maybe I do have it in me. Hopefully, I'll get the chance tomorrow. At the same time, we haven't played our best soccer yet, because we haven't been completely relaxed. But we've had a great week. We're ready and I'm ready if they need me.

Leah: Were you ever overwhelmed by the number of people at a game?

Shannon: No, We've had great friendly crowds cheering for us and that gives us an edge.

Leah: Are you nervous about the game tomorrow?

Shannon: Yeah, I think we're nervous - not a nervousness that's going to affect our play. It's a "good" nervousness and we're definitely ready to go out there and have fun.

Q. This is about Michelle Akers. Are you surprised at how well she's been all along?

Shannon: It doesn't surprise me at all. We see a side of "Mich" others don't see, with the IV sticking out of her arm. She still manages a smile when you walk by. She's got the biggest heart and soul of anyone on the team. It's just a great honor to be able to say I've played with her. I was just joking with her out at the practice. She's got that demanding call for the ball. So, I told her, when I first got on the team she almost made me "pee in my pants"" every time she screamed for it! She said "You're giving me a complex!" But she's just great, so down to earth. She's always there laughing. She's always there for the moment and she's here because she just loves the game. It's her dream, she's been chasing it and she's still on top of her game.

Q. Over the years, is there anything unusual about her determination?

Shannon: Her determination is remarkable. You watch "Mich" after all her surgeries. At the beginning of this year in residency, she broke her cheekbone. She's out for four weeks. We come out to train the next day. There's "Mich" with her training gear and running. We said "Mich, you're out for four weeks." "No," she says. "They're wrong." To see her going against the doctors, but she knew. She is still there and she comes to practice. She's there cheering for us even when she can't train. She's a great leader.

Q. Coming into the locker room after a game, can you discuss how she looks

Shannon: She looks like she's been through a war. After the second game, the Nigeria game, I came in and she was on the table. She was exhausted. She had the IV hanging up and was just laying out. I asked if she wanted anything. I just wanted to tell her she was awesome out there and we definitely needed her. And you get that little smile. She manages to keep that positive spin on things. Not many people would be able to fight what she's gone through time and time again.

Michelle Akers, Midfielder

Q. "Pig Farmer" was one of your aliases for a while. Where did that come from?

Michelle: I have nothing against the Pork Industry! It's a family joke, mostly between my Dad and me. We were watching a documentary on TV and we just started calling each other "Pig Farmer" - it just evolved from there. He's a Marine, so we just go off on those kinds of things.

Q. Michelle, when you're out there, whether in D.C. or in the Rose Bowl tomorrow with 90,000 people in the stands, do you ever think back when there were only 10 people sitting in the stands?

Michelle: I remember back to my childhood days and I was taping my cleats together with athletic tape. Also, seeing the reaction of my father with the media all around, and people asking for my autograph, or reading about me in the paper or watching me on TV, seeing my Dad kind of look at me in a different way is overwhelming at times. He knows me best and to him, I'm still a little girl. For him to see me with all this "stuff" going on around me, being someone other than his little girl, is pretty amazing.

Q. Do you have some mixed emotions because this may possibly be your last World Cup? Any little bit of sadness?

Michelle: No regrets. This is my third World Cup. I've played my heart out. I'm very satisfied with what this team has done and the legacy I will have left World Cup-wise. The parts I will miss - the team and the inter-personal "stuff," but it's not like I'll never see these guys again. I'm very excited and looking forward to the day when I can say, "I'm done! No more fitness! No more training!"

Q. What is your legacy?

Michelle: You're seeing it in the kids' eyes. That won't stop.

Q. Michelle, what do you expect from China tomorrow? You've played them a lot; is this the best they've ever played? They have a lot of reasons for revenge tomorrow.

Michelle: Yes, they do, but so do we. The last game we played them, we lost. As far as their motivation, I don't know. I'm just focusing on what our team needs to do to win tomorrow. Period. I don't care who we're playing. China is an excellent team and we will have to play a great game with 11 players out to win and we are ready to do that.

Q. Will this have to be your best game of the tournament to win?

Michelle: It depends on what kind of team China puts on the field. I'm assuming that they are going to be fired up and playing their best, so we will have to do the same. If we happen to win on a sub-par performance, then it will be because we wanted it more, or we had more heart, and that's kind of been the reason we're here at the Finals in the first place.

Q. Are you still planning to stick it out for the Olympics?

Michelle: I'm strongly considering it. This will be my last World Cup. No way am I going on for the next four years.

Julie Foudy, Midfielder

Q. In '94, did you come to the Men's World Cup games and ever think that five years down the road you'd be here?
Julie: No. Never. But I thought how cool it would be to have the same atmosphere. I watched Columbia here. I watched the Finals but, no, I never would have envisioned this even four years ago.

Q. Did you always think that, if you had the opportunity, you could do it?
Julie: When they first thought about doing this in small venues, we said "No way! You're not giving this team what it deserves and what it's worth." So when they decided to go into big venues, it wasn't as if it wasn't going to be successful. It was right on, the way it should be with a feeling that this is something we can do. We said, "This is a goldmine of personalities and a goldmine of talent and it needed to be promoted better."

July 10, 1999
Under The Press Tent at the Rose Bowl
Pasadena, California

As a junior reporter under the press tent with hundreds of journalists from around the world, I knew I wouldn't be able to really interview anyone. At first, Briana Scurry, Brandi Chastain and Coach Tony DiCicco were up on a small stage, answering questions. Then, other players appeared and were available for comments, so I just went from one player to the next, recording their comments.

Briana Scurry, Hero

Q. After your big save, what were you yelling?
Briana: I was telling them to "C'mon. Make it loud! Loud as you can. Cheer on the team!" I was just a little out of my mind right then. I was really focused on that one shooter and I had a feeling when she was walking up that I could get that one. I don't know how that is, but every now and then, I get that feeling and sure enough, that was the one I got and saved. I was just very excited and I knew that if we could get two more in, we were gonna' bring the Cup home.

Q. What did Tony and you talk about? And who was the woman you went into the stands to hug?
Briana: The first question was "What did Tony and I talk about?" We just basically discussed that he had confidence in me, that I could make the save and I felt good about it. He knew I was confident, and that was my best friend Brandy, who came here and has been here the entire tournament, supporting me with my parents.

Coach Tony DiCicco

Q. How would you rate Briana's tournament?
Coach Tony: Bri has had such a wonderful tournament, she's been for sure one of our key players of the tournament. I just told her that all she could be in the shootout is a hero. There is no way a goalkeeper could be the goat in a penalty kick shootout. The only thing she could be was a hero. Bri WAS the hero.

Brandi Chastain, Hero

Q. When you received your medal, you bowed to the flag. What were you thinking?
Brandi: I was thinking we won it!! The crowd was so supportive. I'm a bit of a ham when it comes to big crowds.

Co-Captain Carla Overbeck under the press tent.

Cindy Parlow, Champion

Q. What did you think about the Chinese team?
Cindy: I've always said that the Chinese are very well organized and they are very tough. There was one or two of their people who would come in very fast, ready to tackle you. They were tough today. It was definitely a "workman's" game instead of a creative game.

Q. Are you glad it's over?
Cindy: Big time. Even if we had taken second place, I think I'm glad it's finally over. We've been waiting for this day so long. It's been crazy and hectic and I'm so glad it is over.

Q. What do you do now?
Cindy: Relax. Rest. Go on a little media blitz. Who knows? We're going to talk about it, try to get back to normal as fast as we can.

Q. What do you think about penalty kicks deciding a game?
Cindy: We think it's a terrible way to go. So many events are won and lost through penalty kicks. The beauty of the game and the people who like to see the game want to see the "legs" of the players. Not too many people can keep going for two, three, four hours. But it's got to be decided in some way.

Q. What was your feeling when they put that medal around your neck?
Cindy: It was one of relief that it's finally over. And one of absolute pride. I'm proud, very proud. I feel really very rewarded. We've been working so hard, training so hard. Its very exciting.

Q. Did weather play a factor? It was hot in the stands. I can imagine how hot it was on the field.
Cindy: Over the course of 90 minutes, yes. How hot it was, takes a toll. Not a huge toll. That's why we train in the heat, to get used to the heat. But it takes its toll.

Q. Did the penalty kicks sell the sport or are there people who think that after 120 minutes . . .?
Cindy: A final match like this when you have two quality teams to sell the game, it's almost that you would like to go down to the wire. It keeps people on the edge. If people need a reason to say they've gotten their money's worth, then that's the reason. If you are a true fan, or even if you're a new fan, you understand the nature of the competition and that's how to win.

Q. What did President Clinton say to you in the locker room?
Cindy: He congratulated us on the win. He actually thanked us for all we've done for America and America's female athletes.

Q. Can you talk about the team's overall effort?
Cindy: Our defense was so incredibly organized today. I think they were the key to the game. They didn't make Bri have to make too many big-time saves. They were very important today.

Q. Any training tomorrow?
Cindy: No training tomorrow, thank God.

Q. Why such a scoreless game? Other times you've played this team, there were two or three goals. Why scoreless today?

Cindy: Both teams came out very strong. Both teams played very well. We were both very organized in attacking. It was just a battle. But with the two best teams in the world, you are not going to see too many goals or too many mistakes. China was great today. I have to give them credit. They stopped our attack. We would have liked to finish in 90 minutes, but we weren't able to. But we did what we had to do, to get the job done.

Q. How is this different from when you won the Olympics?

Cindy: The only thing that's different now, is that Women's Soccer is on the stage. The Olympics are a lot of different sports, but we are on the stage now. People are coming out, people are watching on TV, people are reading about us in the newspapers. They're reading about women's soccer and women's soccer only right now. It's not really about the other sports that are in the Olympics. This is a really big day for us. A dream come true for all 20 of us - 20 plus, including the staff and everyone involved with the team. We knew it was going to be close. It was amazing. The fans were great, very enthusiastic and energetic. We couldn't have asked for anything better.

Marla Messing, President / CEO, Women's World Cup

Q. This tournament was a total success. Can you estimate the surplus you expect from it?

Marla Messing: First of all, it will probably take eight to ten weeks to have a pretty good idea of what the surplus is. It could take a year to absolutely pinpoint it. We still don't know what the exact surplus is of the 1994 World Cup. There are always these lingering things. But I think that within eight to ten weeks we will have a pretty good idea of what it generated.

Q. Five years ago, Alan (Rothenberg, Chairman of the Board) always mentioned "Lightning in a Bottle." Is this a bigger deal than that was?

Marla Messing: I think in some ways, it is a bigger deal, because the 1994 World Cup always had the "history." There was never any doubt that it was going to be successful on some level. This "Lightning in a Bottle" tournament came out from nowhere. Aside from the people who spent years working on it, the American public was introduced to it rather late in the game and how they embraced it, I think, in some ways, is rather unprecedented.

Q. What's the future for Women's Soccer?

Marla Messing: What I see in the future is one very important tournament every four years, such as the Women's World Cup. We're going to have huge numbers of young girls register for soccer and want to play recreational soccer or organized soccer and if the groundswell continues, hopefully, in a couple of years, we'll have the resources to start a professional soccer league.

Q. This is now just in the "hopeful stage," but wasn't U.S. Soccer talking about getting one going in 2000? Are they looking at a study?

Marla Messing: Yes. But you need investors. You need sponsors and, in this day and age, you need TV. You also need to create something that's authentic so people like you will cover it. There's a lot of work to be done. I think right now it is a hope, a dream, but I know they're to work on it and they're spending money to invest in it.

Q. Is there any profit money earmarked for a league like there was from '94?

Marla Messing: No, not like there was in '94 when there was a very specific sum set aside to seed a league. That doesn't exist. But we are going to have a surplus and our hope is that that money is going to go to the future of Women's Soccer.

Julie Foudy, Co-Captain, Champion

Q. Do you realize what you've done for young women, the girls of America?

Julie: Yes, we've talked about it a lot. We always knew that this tournament transcended soccer; it was about a bigger message. We got a lot of criticism from soccer die-hards who said, "But this is the World Cup! This is about soccer!" Yes, it is, but there are so many girls out there, it's also about hope, watching women do great things in front of great crowds. It's about them finally realizing, "I can do it too." I think that's such a great message for all young girls, and even boys, to see that. So this is something we take very seriously and we've talked a lot about it being the greater message for this tournament.

Q. The WNBA has made great inroads, but it seems that soccer is THE team sport for women in America and you guys have proved it.

Julie: I think there are so many kids who play soccer in this country. There are about seven million girls and as many boys. We have a great fan base out there and what is so attractive is that it's such a great team. It's not about one player, or two players but 20 individuals who collectively make an awesome team. That's always been our greatest strength. I think fans see that and are attracted to that.

Q. When you were standing on the podium after winning the match, did you get an eerie feeling that it wasn't real or were you grounded in reality?

Julie: No, I was "psyched." We've talked about this for so long that being up there was very realistic. We come into every tournament expecting to be on that podium and it was just great. I had about 500 relatives in the audience, my husband, my parents. To me, that was the best moment I could give back to them as a thank you.

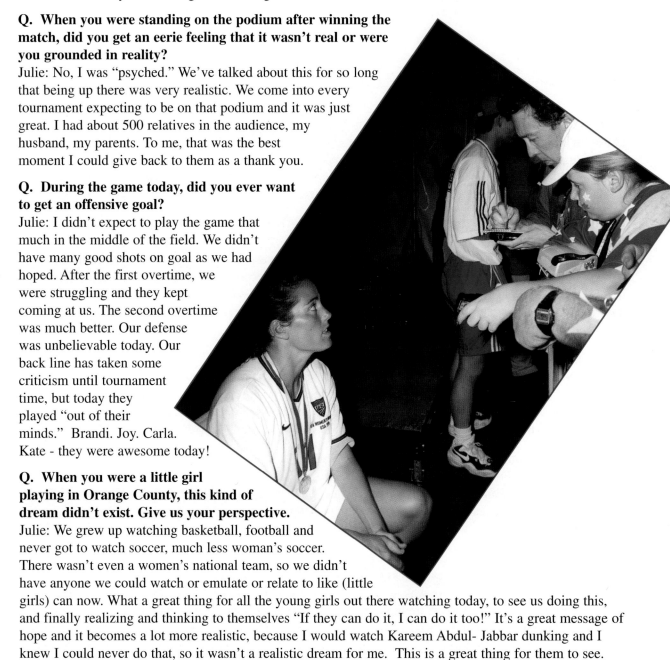

Q. During the game today, did you ever want to get an offensive goal?

Julie: I didn't expect to play the game that much in the middle of the field. We didn't have many good shots on goal as we had hoped. After the first overtime, we were struggling and they kept coming at us. The second overtime was much better. Our defense was unbelievable today. Our back line has taken some criticism until tournament time, but today they played "out of their minds." Brandi. Joy. Carla. Kate - they were awesome today!

Q. When you were a little girl playing in Orange County, this kind of dream didn't exist. Give us your perspective.

Julie: We grew up watching basketball, football and never got to watch soccer, much less woman's soccer. There wasn't even a women's national team, so we didn't have anyone we could watch or emulate or relate to like (little girls) can now. What a great thing for all the young girls out there watching today, to see us doing this, and finally realizing and thinking to themselves "If they can do it, I can do it too!" It's a great message of hope and it becomes a lot more realistic, because I would watch Kareem Abdul- Jabbar dunking and I knew I could never do that, so it wasn't a realistic dream for me. This is a great thing for them to see.

Q. What's it going to take to launch a league?

Julie: Obviously it's very positive. It shows we have a fan base, but at the same time, realistically, this is a World Cup and it's created a lot of enthusiasm, but it's going to take a lot of work to put together a first-rate league. The Olympics will help because we'll be in the spotlight again for another year, but it's a necessity that we remain on top.

Q. Six months ago the "craziness" began. I don't know how many thousands of miles you've logged since, but you were happy then. You're exhausted now. How does the happiness match up?

Julie: I'm exhausted but happy. We've put so many hours behind this as our goal, and when you become a soccer player, the Olympics are fantastic, but the pinnacle of a soccer player's career is the World Cup. We lost in '95 and we made an oath never to let it happen again, and we are elated to have won it back here in the United States.

Q. How did it feel to be on top of the podium?

Julie: You dream about it for so long. Being on that podium you think about it and you look at the Olympics and think about that podium. And you take that last step and think "O.K. I'm here!" and after all those dreams and hours of work you're on top of that podium. It's a feeling no one can take away. We worked our "butts" off and we're here.

Q. What's the greatest legacy of the past three weeks?

Julie: I think that one of the greatest legacies is that they were going to do it in small stadiums on the East Coast. They weren't going to do it first-class. Instead, at the last minute, they decided to take a risk. Still, everyone said "You can't do it. It's not going to work." At our press conference in February for the All-Star match, people were saying "Are you kidding? You're downsizing the stadiums. This is ridiculous." There were a lot of doubters out there, and still, they were able to put on this historic event. That's such a great message to the kids. That's always been the case of this team. Obstacles thrown in front of us. "You can't do it. You can't win. It's not going to draw." But we always seem to rise to the occasion. I love that message to the kids! If they tell you "you can't," just smile, and say "you can." Take a risk, because risk brings rewards.

Q. Compare winning the Cup today to '91, what is the difference?

Julie: We weren't supposed to win in '91. That was the first World Cup we went into and the U.S. wasn't even "on the map" for soccer then. We kind of did it by storm and through guts. We weren't a great team, but we were a good team. We hadn't really trained together. We were young. And now it seems harder. The journey's been harder. We've had a lot of pressure on us to carry this tournament. There were a lot of people who thought we couldn't do it, but we prevailed. It just seemed harder this time around.

Tiffeny Milbrett, Champion

Q. Did you think that this would be the enormous success it turned out to be?

Tiffeny: I thought it would always be an enormous success, but it has exceeded my expectations. When I sat in Giant Stadium, on Saturday, June 19, for the opening game with over 78,000 people, I new we had a hit on our hands.

Q. Did you feel the same as the games progressed?

Tiffeny: I told someone earlier this week that I had this re-curring nightmare. This tournament was so much like the '94 Men's World Cup right down to the USA-Brazil game at Stanford Stadium. I was so concerned that this final match would not pay off and it's amazing that there is this 0-0 game and yet, it does pay off. I mean, it was a phenomenal match, the fans were on the edge of their seats, and it just goes to show you, the score isn't really what matters. It's how the match was played, and this was wildly different from the Italy-Brazil game five years ago.

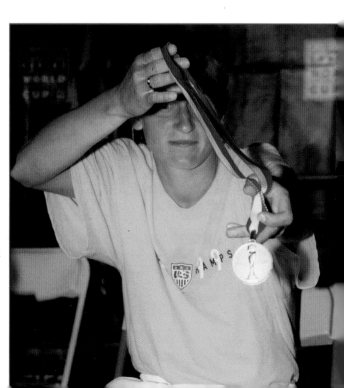

Kate Sobrero, Champion

Q. How many minutes did Michelle Akers play? 80 minutes?
Kate: It was incredible with the heat out there. We couldn't have done it without her.

Q. What did Coach Tony say to you at halftime?
Kate: He said we had "45 minutes to accomplish our dream and we better go out and do it now and we won't have any regrets for our hard work over the past six months. No team has worked harder than us." That's so true. He said "It's your dream and it's up to you."

Q. If you "guys" were looking for the best performers of all the teams, who would it be?
Kate: China is a great team. I think we always played well against them. It wasn't the "showy" soccer we're used to but it was good. The Chinese attack as a team and they all go together. They always keep their numbers around the ball, so you're never going to feel like you're under siege. It takes them a while to build up, but they get ahead. There were a lot of times we were just totally on the defense. We had to keep our eyes open. They were definitely attacking us pretty hard, but we were able to combat it.

Q. Do they have the best defensive players of the countries you've played against?
Kate: Yes. They are a quality team. I think we played very well and we didn't want to let any breakdowns happen. No one really had a clear shot at a goal for most of the game. The one time, the corner kick.

Q. What about Michelle?
Kate: She's with the doctor, getting an IV. She'll be totally fine.

Q. Where did you get the energy after 90 minutes?
Kate: I don't know. I'm pretty sore right now, but I felt that if I didn't give 100 percent right then, I'd relive that memory. Our psychologist told us that every few minutes, if you're dead tired, just tell yourself "two more minutes." That's what I kept saying to myself, "two more minutes, two more minutes." I just kept doing it.

Q. What did you think when you were awarded a World Cup Final penalty kick?
Kate: God, please don't make me take one! Honestly, I didn't want to take one. I wanted to say "get me out of here!" I'm number 10 and I hoped someone would make it before me. I just hoped the best for Bri. She was the one at the greatest disadvantage. To have the poise of the other five shooters on our team was unbelievable. I couldn't have had that poise.

Krístíne Lílly, Champíon

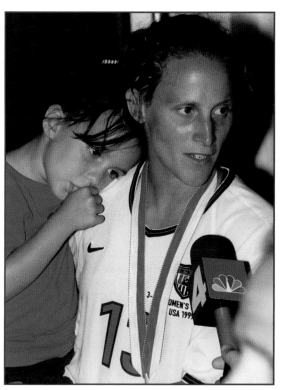

Kristine serves as babysitter for Kate Fawcett.

Q. I may be wrong but, it seems that the team isn't celebrating, but rather relieved. Is that the case?
Kristine: Just wait until you see us tonight! Then you'll see us celebrating. But there is a sense of relief. It's been an intense six months. A lot of media. A lot of focus on this group. You know. . . carrying the banner for Women's Soccer. All along we understood the bigger picture of what it would mean for us to win this. Awww, look at Kate. Wanna sit on my lap so you can go to sleep? You okay, Kate? . . .Okay.

Q. Was Michelle aware of what happened at the end?
Kristine: Oh yes. Very aware . . . in the locker room.

Q. What was the feeling when she went off the field? She'd been playing so hard all day.
Kristine: You know when Michelle goes off she just can't go anymore. It's not like maybe she can go another 10 minutes. When Michelle's done, she's done. She can hit the wall. So obviously, there's a sense of loss, but you know she's given everything she's got and you have to adjust to it. It's happened a lot before in games so we're used to it, but anytime Michelle steps off the field, it's a loss.

Q. Even though you've had big crowds all the way with every stadium a sellout, when you went out on the field today here at the Rose Bowl, was it a different feeling than in the past?
Kristine: It was awesome. When I walked on the field, I got tears in my eyes, the feeling was overwhelming! It was a different feeling from the other games just to know that this was the Final. And the crowd was awesome - this was the biggest crowd ever to watch a women's sports event.

Q. Comment on the corner kick that you headed off the line to save the game in overtime.
Kristine: I was just doing my job. If I didn't head it, I think I would have looked stupid.

Q. At the time, did you realize how important that save was?
Kristine: No. I really didn't. I just wanted to try to support the others. I just wanted overtime to be over.

Q. On the way in, I passed a group of Number 13's; it looked like a Lilly Family Reunion.
Kristine: I have about 25 people here. Immediate family, cousins, friends, so it was probably them.

Q. Was the header off the line the biggest non-goal achievement you've accomplished in soccer?
Kristine: I guess so. Man, that was so awesome! But it was right at my head. If I missed it, I would have looked stupid. So I was on the post. One of my jobs is to cover the goal with Bri.

Q. Do you have any flashbacks like Mike Burns of the U.S. Men's National Team who was in a similar predicament in the World Cup last summer?
Kristine: No, not really. But I was glad to be there. I'm just glad that we won. The PK's were awesome. China's a great team. They're a classy team. You had two of the best teams in the world right there.

Q. We all knew that this was going to be a brutally tough game, but did you think it was going to go 120 minutes with PK's?
Kristine: I hoped it wouldn't, but I knew how good China is and how good we are. When you have two teams that play excellent defense, this is what happens. We held strong, finished the PK's we had to. It's awesome.

Q. So what do you do now?
Kristine: Relax, man! Hang around the West Coast for a bit and totally relax.

July 11, 1999
Victory Rally
Los Angeles, California

When we arrived at the Victory Rally, all the players were in a room with security guards keeping fans out. I heard they were doing more interviews, so I asked my parents if I could try for some more comments from the players. They agreed it was a good idea, so I made my way through the small crowd of fans to the security woman. She immediately told me the room was off-limits to fans, so I showed her my media credentials. She was pretty surprised as she let me into the wide open room. Guess she had never seen a 12 year-old junior reporter.

Joy Fawcett, Defender, Champion, and Soccer Mom

Q. Were your children at the game yesterday?
Joy: Yes, but they looked awful, because their dad had dressed them. My mom helped them out with that in the World Cup, so I wasn't too worried. I always pick them out in the stands, every game. They will wave, they will get all excited that I wave.

Q. How do they support you?
Joy: I think the biggest support they give me, is that they're so adjustable that they make me feel that I'm not hindering their lives. They're not put out by everything that's going on, they are so easy going. If I felt that I was hurting their lives, I wouldn't be doing this, so the fact that they go with the flow and they make it that easy for me, with traveling, and everything.

Q. How do they do that?
Joy: I don't think they consciously do that, they just enjoy being with me and not have me leaving them back behind. They are just happy to be there, with the whole group.

Q. Did they celebrate with you last night?
Joy: They came to the post-game party and they were just out, 'cause they were so tired. They had been up since 6 in the morning and they were just exhausted.

Q. They fell asleep at the party?
Joy: They came down to the field and I had to go do drug testing, so I let them go with the team. They played with the team, and then they were just out, because they were so tired.

Q. What time did they go to bed?
Joy: By the time we got there, it was about eight.

Q. What about you, what time did you go to bed?
Joy: Ummm. . . three. We had a sitter for the night, so my husband and I went out with the team and we went dancing.

Q. Where did you go? Was it private or did you go to a club?
Joy: It was private in the beginning, then adidas put on a little private bar, they closed down a bar for us. It was fun!

Q. What would you say to women as role models to their daughters in sports?
Joy: I think it's just neat that they can see what I've done. Just that they are a part of my life, so they can see what their life can be like, how many choices that they have. Whatever they want to be. I think that's something my daughter can grasp, I could see her grasp over time, because she's been traveling since she was born. She's five now. In the beginning, she wanted to be a cooker at McDonald's. Then she's like, "Well, maybe I want to be a soccer player during the day and a cooker at night. Is that okay Mommy?" "That's fine, you can do whatever!" It was neat to see her change, knowing that she wanted to do more things.

Q. It never occurred to you to stop playing after having children?

Joy: No I love kids, and I didn't want to be older to have kids. I knew I wanted to play. I had talked to the coach and told him, "I want to get pregnant. Is it okay if they travel with me?" He was like "Fine!" I think if you want something, you can do it, and work out a way. I had to pay for my kid's flights and the nanny's flights, and my own room in the beginning. It was tough on our income, because we don't make that much anyway. But as things progressed, U.S. Soccer picked up the tab eventually, and paid for the nanny and the kid's flights.

Q. What do you think this does for women's sports?

Joy: I think it's opened a lot of people's eyes that have never seen women's sports, or women's soccer. But they used to think it wasn't very physical or very fun to watch. But when you watch the women's game, you see how physical it is, how fast paced it is, it's really not, soccer-wise, that different.

Q. What happens next?

Joy: Well, we've got this long schedule, we're very busy. Hopefully, we'll all just take a break and regenerate, so that when we come back, we are fresh and ready to go again.

Q. Do you think you'll stay together?

Joy: For the Olympics, yeah. We all have to make the team, so we have to try out again.

Q. How do you keep your confidence up during a game if you make a mistake?

Joy: A lot of self-talk, to boost my confidence, I block out the negative or replace it with good thoughts.

Q. When you make a mistake, you do what?

Joy: I'll be mad about it, but then I won't dwell on it. I think about the play that is at hand.

Q. You're able to that?

Joy: Yeah, it's something you learn. You learn that over time. When I was younger, I couldn't do that.

Carla Overbeck, Captain, Defender and Soccer Mom

Q. Are you surprised with the level of support you've received from the public?

Carla: We're just excited that people are passionate about our sport, because we're very passionate about it. It's nice to know that people want to get involved and be part of it.

Q. Do you feel overwhelmed right now?

Carla: Well, a little bit, but you know we were just at Disneyland and we were on floats parading down Main Street and it's so exciting that people are aware of our team first of all, and that they just want to be a part of it, and for us, that's a great deal.

Q. Is there a victory tour planned?

Carla: Well, we've been handed sort of a tentative schedule.

Q. Already?

Carla: Yeah, we're going to go back this tour for a couple of weeks, and then hopefully, the leadership on this team will get together with the federation and start the ground work for starting the Olympics. The media is going to be great the next couple of weeks, and if we can get something into place where we are playing in front of the public, obviously people want to come out to watch us play and that's a good thing. That will help us prepare, help us get ready for the future and for 2000.

Julie Foudy, Legend

As I approached Julie to tell her she was "Foudious" in yesterday's game, I heard an announcement that the rally was about to begin. A reporter looked towards me and asked Julie one last question:

Q. Hey, who's this?

Julie: Oh, that's Leah. She's the best of the bunch of ya!!

CONGRATULATIONS!

1999 World Cup Champions